I0108190

PURPOSEFUL PARENTING

PURPOSEFUL PARENTING

A Journey

JOY C. OGUCHI

Copyright © 2016 Joy C. Oguchi
All rights reserved.
No portion of this book may be reproduced in any form or by any means for commer-
cial gain or profit without the written permission of the publisher and the author.

ISBN-13: 9780692653395
ISBN-10: 0692653392

All Bible quotations are taken from the New King James Version (NKJV) of the Holy Bible.

While the author has made every effort to provide accurate Internet addresses at the
time of publication, neither the publisher nor the author assumes any responsibility
for errors, or changes that occur after publication. Further, the publisher or author
does not have any control over and does not assume any responsibility for third-party
websites or their content.

FOREWORD

PURPOSEFUL PARENTING IS a must read for all parents and even parents-to-be. For parents, irrespective of the age of the child, there is something in this book for you. For parents-to-be, this book lays a solid foundation as you prepare to build your own family and for grandparents, it helps you understand the changing times and the dynamics of bringing up a child in today's world.

The author has brought out very important issues that affect parenting today, in a simple down-to-earth manner that completely removes all forms of complexities and confusion in parenting. She has used real life examples of her family and has brought to the fore the changing times that we live in. Not only has she made the book simple, she has made it easy to read, not as a hard and fast rule, but with principles to guide and direct, knowing that each child is unique and each environment is different.

Having watched Joy grow from childhood and seen her pass through the various life stages to motherhood and also watched with excitement the diligence with which she is raising her children and contributing to the lives of other children around her, I do not hesitate to recommend Purposeful Parenting to every one, both young and old. It is not a book of "do as I say" but a practical book born out of experience. The author has not only grown through the principles she has shared in this book, she is also working them and the results are evident.

Don't just buy this book for your shelf; read, meditate and put it to work. The building of a new generation is the work of everyone and this book will show you how to play your part well and leave a legacy in the sands of time.

I congratulate Joy for taking the bold step of putting down these age-long truths and I look forward to reading testimonials from lives touched by this book.

Shalom.

Bishop Peace Okonkwo
Resident Pastor, TREM Headquarters
Lagos, Nigeria

Praise for Purposeful Parenting

PURPOSEFUL PARENTING BY Joy C. Oguchi is intentional and strategically written with both mums and dads in mind. Mrs. Oguchi has been able to systematically utilize her vast travel experience and knowledge of the intricacies of international and domestic family life to produce a book that answers to all cultures and deep Christian values.

I am endorsing and highly recommending Purposeful Parenting for newly weds, soon to be parents, families preparing for teenage parenting, grandparents, teachers and those called to minister to children and teenagers. The information in the book is incredibly vast.

Rev. Marjorie O. Esomowei
President Wisdom for Women International, UK

Purposeful Parenting can be said to be a case study of the Author, Mrs. Joy Oguchi and her journey from childhood, being parented to becoming a parent herself. It is certainly an interesting, practical and easy book to read. It is extremely informative and engaging. Enjoy.

Mrs. Kehinde Nwani
MD/CEO Meadow Hall Group, Nigeria
(Founder, Meadow Hall School)

Purposeful Parenting is an in-depth look at parenting, which has become a serious challenge in our generation and the nation. I like the way the author has looked at both the spiritual and the practical aspect of parenting which can be applied across board.

I pray that this book will get into the hands of all those who will find it useful and that there will be a way of getting it to young couples who can read it before they are faced with the challenges. In fact, every family will be blessed by it.

Pastor (Mrs.) Laolu Adefarasin
Guiding Light Assembly, Lagos, Nigeria

DEDICATION

I dedicate this book to my lovely children; Ebubechukwu, Uchechukwu and Amarachukwu and to my wonderful parents - Elder Joseph & Deaconess Matilda Ezeagwula, whose footprints I am still tracing.

ACKNOWLEDGEMENT

A SPECIAL "THANK you" to my loving husband, Theophilus Oguchi, whose encouragement and support birthed this work.

Many thanks to Tochi Eze, Iretijabarr Ghatekha-Ogbomo, Ugochukwu Ezeagwula and everyone who contributed in any way to this work.

TABLE OF CONTENTS

INTRODUCTION

I STRONGLY BELIEVE that every child can be great and that this can only be attained with proper guidance. God entrusted His children to us as parents so we can guide them into His purpose, as they cannot pilot themselves. Children cannot attain their highest potential without proper guidance from their parents and other concerned adults around them as they go through the journey of life. We are their "destiny helpers."

As a parent, I desire to see my children succeed and reach their fullest potential. The overwhelming realization that I influence their lives for good, bad, or worse (if I choose to be indifferent) inspired me to write this book. After years of research, I've been able to pinpoint four different perspectives on parenting: where parenting is seen as a journey, a process, a ministry, and a purpose-driven path.

- **A Journey:** We may not know the outcome until we get to the end of the journey, but we can be sure of our destination if we commit ourselves to doing it right.
- **A Process:** Parenting is a process that starts from the womb and goes through adolescence and into adulthood.
- **A Ministry:** As a ministry, our primary mandate is to raise children according to God's standards by meeting their physical, emotional, intellectual, and spiritual needs without compromising the standards of God.
- **A Purpose-Driven Path:** God has a definite purpose for every child, and as parents we have to discover and understand the purpose of God to be able to parent accordingly.

My life and my views of parenting changed when I realized that God is counting on us to become a positive influence on the future of every child He brings along our path. The future of the next generation is subject to our influence today.

I've volunteered as a Sunday school teacher for over twenty-three years and am the biological mother of three children, as well as being a counselor and an educator. Thus, I have a wide range of experiences with children at different stages of their development. Over the years I've identified that children need proper nurturing in order to attain their maximum potential as intended by God.

Our world today is full of perversions and a lot of negative influences on children (through unguarded media, the Internet, and peer pressure, among others). One of the best ways children are protected against perverse influences is by having a strong, positive, involved parent in their lives—a child-attached relationship. However, we cannot lead our children without knowing where we are going. Therefore, it becomes necessary for each of us to discover what God expects of us and what direction He is leading us in our parenting journey.

I can assure you that parenting is a very interesting, fulfilling, and rewarding experience, though very demanding. It is a wonderful privilege to be chosen by God to bring precious lives into this world and be given the divine responsibility of nurturing them into responsible and God-fearing adults. *Purposeful Parenting* is intended to help you reflect on and discover:

- your purpose as a parent and the purpose you are called to achieve in the lives of your children and, by extension, in our world
- your parenting ministry and the joy that comes from serving (your) children
- your unique parenting process (the journey), as there is *no single right way* to raise children and so you need to develop your own process as you go through your journey

Whether you have an infant, a toddler, a growing child, or an adolescent (or if you are a single man or woman who desires to be a parent someday), *Purposeful Parenting* is written with you in mind: to help you discover your purpose and develop your process in bringing out the best in your wonderful children. If you are a working mother struggling to make time for your children, a homemaker not finding enough time for yourself, or a busy dad who has to make frequent trips on the job, you will receive the knowledge and strength to parent your children purposefully, with the kind of passion that will help you maximize your available time and resources, and give you the grace to move through the parenting journey with joy and a strong sense of fulfillment.

When you discover your purpose and the direction of your journey, allowing God to lead you and letting Him perfect His work and the walk, you will see yourself raising amazing children and invariably making the world a better place. God bless you as you read on.

—Joy C. Oguchi, 2016

1

CHILDHOOD BACKGROUND: LESSONS FROM MY PARENTS!

Everything depends on upbringing.

—LEO TOLSTOY

I WAS BROUGHT up in the metropolitan city of Lagos, in Nigeria, in a home filled with love and discipline. Living with five sisters and two brothers, one would expect life to be chaotic, especially since we weren't affluent, but we grew together in love and faith to become a very close-knit family.

We were a family with different gifts and talents, and with different challenges, too. Each one of the eight of us had (and still has) our unique challenges, but in love, we have been able to stick together: telling one another the truth even when it hurts, sharing in one another's challenges, celebrating one another's victories, and simply being there for one another.

This is not to say we were a "perfect" family; as a matter of fact, there is no such thing as a perfect family. Even though, like many great families out there, we had testimonies of great successes as a family, we also had our challenges and shortcomings. However, it is important to me as I raise my children that I have a model to emulate as they grow together in love and faith—preferably, the model I found in the family I grew up in.

My life today is directly influenced by my upbringing and the hard work of purposeful parents, for whom I am ever grateful to God. Hence, when I look back, I see my mistakes, errors, omissions, and commissions as part of my learning process. I have no regrets whatsoever in life. It is therefore my desire that my children (and children in general) also grow up without regrets. I consistently pray that God will help me give my children adequate guidance through their journey to help them make the right decisions in their own lives.

My Mum

Mum was a teacher who devoted her life to loving and caring for all the children God brought her way, starting with her own. Those days, teachers, especially in the public sector, were often not well paid, and their welfare was neglected. They were sometimes not paid for several months, even after working so hard. Despite all odds, Mum was passionate about her job. I remember saying over and over that I would never be a teacher or have anything to do with education and the school system, especially when I watched how much she put into the job while receiving so little in terms of compensation.

At that time, teachers were forced to compromise in their duties, and due to the low salaries, they grew nonchalant. Many of them became businesswomen. Rather than devoting themselves to the teaching and learning of/for their students, they spent their time buying and selling on school grounds to make extra money to augment salaries that were often delayed. Although, my mum understood the concept of multiple streams of income and also had a petty business through which she managed to make extra money for our family, she never sold anything on school grounds or during her work hours. She devoted herself to teaching the children in her care, and that gave her a great deal of fulfillment.

Once I asked my mum why she continued to teach, knowing that she was not making much out of it. Her answer was something I pondered for a long time but couldn't make sense of. She said to me; "Joy, teaching is a calling for me. I believe God has called me to help Him build the world."

Build the world? I was taught in Sunday school that right at the beginning, God created the heavens and the earth. So I wondered how Mum would help God build a world that He (God) had already created. At the end of creation, He looked at all He made and saw that they were good. Mum's response stuck with me until I was old enough to understand what she meant by "building the world." To the glory of God, today I have joined her in this business of building the world for God: one child at a time, *starting from my home.*

In response to my question, Mum further explained to me that through teaching she was sowing a seed into our future (the future of her children). Again, this did not make any sense to me at that moment. I probably was too young to understand deep sayings. But one thing I knew as far back as I can remember: my parents had a plan. They were on a journey heading somewhere. They knew what they wanted for their children, and they had a purpose in mind in everything they did.

Mum often told the story of how she had a scholarship to be trained as a secretary but somehow God ordered her steps into teaching, and she found that teaching gave her fulfillment and the time to be there for her children. Mum told me that being a teacher and especially having the opportunity to have her children in the school with her gave her the opportunity to nurture us all day. And truthfully, I remember those days: my mum paved the way for us in everything. This helped us live consistent lifestyles because we were right under my mother's nose at all times. So for her, it was not all about working to make money but more about the opportunity she had to be right there when we needed her.

Indeed, she had a purpose in mind, and that purpose motivated her to look beyond the fact that she was not compensated well enough for her hard work. She focused on her purpose and the journey. My mum was blessed to have had a job that gave her all that time with us. If you do not have such a "luxury" due to the challenging demands of living in today's world, don't feel condemned. You will find the grace and strategy to reach your goal.

MY DAD

Dad also started off as a teacher. He taught for several years but retired early and ventured into business to see if he could make "ends meet" and to ensure they would not have "all their eggs in one basket," since each time the salaries of teachers were delayed, no income came to our family. However, he ended up as a minister of the gospel.

My parents made it clear what their purpose for parenting was. Dad would often say to us: "We may not be rich in material wealth, but my goal is to ensure that you are rich in spirit and in strength." He told us repeatedly, that one thing he would commit his life to was ensuring we had "Christ and education." At the time I started hearing about "Christ and education," I didn't have a clue what Dad meant, but I heard it over and over. It was like casting a vision: you have to cast it over and over until it becomes a part of the people. For example, I won't forget the scripture: *"Now godliness with contentment is great gain."* (1 Timothy 6:6). I heard this scripture over and over from my parents growing up.

One day after my dad mentioned giving us "Christ and education," my older sister decided to ask him what he meant by his statement. We were already Christians, and we went to Sunday school, sang in the children's choir, and did well academically, and so she demanded an explanation. Dad called for a family meeting one beautiful Saturday morning to explain what he meant. He told us that Christ was the most important component we needed in our lives to succeed and that like-wise education would open doors to those opportunities we needed to succeed in life. He said to us that with Christ, by knowing and ac-cepting Jesus as our Lord and savior and giving Him charge over our lives and education (which by his explanation meant longing for and acquiring knowledge to the very best of our abilities), we would survive anything that life brought our way. In other words, we would be well equipped for life.

"Christ" in our family and by the standards of the Bible represented faith and moral character. Integrity was one of the moral characters that were so often emphasized in our home—so much so that integrity became a "member of our household." Sometimes I still hear my dad's voice echoing in my ears: "Your *yes* must be *yes* and your *no* must be *no*." We were taught humility, perseverance, tolerance, respect, truthfulness, and more.

GROWING UP

When I was growing up, my family was one of the most exciting aspects of my life. My parents ran a "democratic system," where we were all free to express ourselves. I grew up in the days when children could not talk to adults; they were often hushed when they wanted to say something, and many parents preached, "do as I say." The case was very different in our family. Everyone had a chance to talk and share his or her views on issues. Sometimes Dad even gave us debate topics, based on what was going on in society, and allowed us to go research and then come back with our arguments and talk about it at one of our very exciting family gatherings. We shared jokes and laughed together, and we played board games together like Ludo, Scrabble, Monopoly, and card games—noth-ing sophisticated like the electronic games we have today. I remember when it was Mum and Dad's turn to play against each other, we (the chil-dren) would take sides, and some of us would change camps along the way, depending on who was most likely to win. Many times Dad would defeat Mum, and she would always say in a wobbling voice: "*It's a game!*"

We often had formal family meetings, where Dad would prepare an agenda and one of the children would take the minutes of the meeting. This may sound funny and strange, but it was all part of my parents' strategy to instill confidence in us and prepare us for life. (Is it any wonder that almost every member of my family served as leaders and officers in our youth groups and campus fellowships at different times?) At these meetings, we discussed issues that affected our family. Our parents wanted to hear our opinions.

I remember when one of my younger siblings gained admission into one of the federal government colleges in the northern part of Nigeria. This was at a time when there was a religious crisis in the north. We met to discuss it and to consider other alternatives. In the end, the whole family decided that she would stay in Lagos and attend another model college that she had also received an invitation to. Although my sister had looked forward to attending a boarding school and had worked very hard, she was as happy with the family's decision as we all were.

Dad's strategy was to get every member of the family to share a sense of ownership in the family structure: to help us understand that we were all stakeholders in our family, we were all on the journey together, and whatever happened to one of us affected the family as a unit.

BIRTHDAYS

Whenever any family member's birthday neared, we met to discuss what to do. Our parents could not afford to throw birthday parties for us often; however, in spite of this, birthdays were very special moments in our family and still are. Mum and Dad were very transparent, so we knew when they had extra cash and when they didn't. Based on the situation in our family at the time, we would discuss and agree on an affordable way to make the birthday very special for the individual, and we often came up with good ideas of things we could do together as a family.

One thing we did quite often was to have dinner together at home, with the celebrant choosing the menu for the evening. This was really special, and even when the celebrant was not there (usually in school or had traveled), we celebrated birthdays in absentia. This birthday dinner tradition still holds in my father's house, even for those children who are married today. In fact, these celebrations of our birthdays have expanded to include our spouses and children. So with eight biological children, nine grandchildren, four sons-in-law, two daughters-in-law, and two other members of the household who have become part of the children, there is always an opportunity for celebration in my father's house throughout the year, despite very modest budgets.

OUR FAITH

The Christian faith is the foundation upon which our family was built. Faith is the most important component and the bedrock of our family. Faith for us was not just about going to church but also about character and knowing Christ for ourselves.

Going to church was, however, very important to us. We all went to church together as a family. We were a community of faith, and our faith was in Christ Jesus. Everything our parents did was backed up by the word of God. We didn't only go to church, but it was also important that we were committed and served in our local church. We had to prayerfully decide on a ministry in which to serve, even when we were very young. Dad and Mum taught us that worship is not complete without service and giving, and like Jesus, we were called to serve. So we had the opportunity to serve right from the children's church. We all sang in the children's choir, and some of us later joined the adult choir, while others joined the ushers/greeters group, drama group, etc. We also got involved in evangelism.

I remember a time when one of my sisters just couldn't think of a ministry to join. At that time in her life, she was dealing with adolescence and peer pressure. After our family devotion one morning, Dad placed her on a fast and gave her three days to decide on a ministry. Dad and Mum joined her during this period of fasting, and after three days, she announced to the family that she'd been led to join the choir. She went ahead and joined the choir immediately, and God started a great work in her life. She became more focused and had fewer distractions. That, for some reason, brought about a drastic and rapid spiritual growth for her, and she became the prayer warrior of our house and was in charge of our family devotion. We often jokingly called her "our family's prayer contractor."

FAMILY ALTAR

I did not quite appreciate why we had to wake up at 5:00 a.m. every morning to pray in my father's house until I went to boarding school. There my faith was tested, and I began to appreciate the spiritual foundation I'd been given. Morning devotion was another matter that could not be legislated in our household, but my dad was full of humor. I remember when we would all gather for our morning devotion and sleep during the whole thing. Dad and Mum tried different strategies to keep us awake, including making us stand throughout the devotion, but some of us "could sleep on water" and still slept throughout the devotion (and still tried to prove later that we were not sleeping).

So one day Dad announced that he was not going to lead prayers; he asked us to take comfortable positions and just pray individually until we had a release. As each person was done praying, he or she could get up and begin to prepare for the day. Every one of us took the kneeling position, and trust me, almost every one of us literarily went back to bed in that position. Once Dad and Mum finished praying, they got up and went to prepare for the day. One by one, we woke up from our sleep, but no one was allowed to tap anybody. Believe me, some of us were still "fervently praying" while others were already on their way to school. Dad succeeded in proving to those who slept during prayers (and then denied it) that they were indeed sleeping. That day it became obvious, and nobody could argue.

I find the saying "A family that prays together, stays together" to be true. At our family altar, we were able to bond together as we learned to take our individual and family needs and challenges to God in prayer. We experienced the faithfulness of God as a family. We were blessed with answered prayers, we saw mountains move for us, and today I know for sure that God indeed answers prayers.

LESSONS LEARNED

You may wonder why I've provided such a detailed story about my family. I have always believed in reference points. To the glory of God, Mum and Dad's parenting approach, strategy, process, and journey have become a reference point for me because whatever they did obviously worked and they are gladly enjoying the reward. I wanted to give a brief background of my upbringing to help you understand where I am coming from and why I am so passionate about parenting and motherhood.

God gave me extraordinary parents for whom I will always be grateful. Growing up under my mother's guidance, I've come to associate parenting and motherhood with love, selflessness, commitment, availability, and patience. My dad also played a huge part in my life. They were strict on morals and were committed to keeping us within the "straight and narrow." Dad was a disciplinarian and a great encourager, too. He never believed there was anything we couldn't achieve if we set our minds to it, so he made sure we did our best.

I have learned many lessons from my upbringing. The most important one I would like to share at this point is that *purposeful parenting* is sacrifice. It requires selflessness. In today's world, so many things demand our attention as well as that of our children. We will explore this further later in the book, but at this point you must see *purposeful parenting* as a sacrifice you must make to direct your children on the path of life.

MY PARENTING PURPOSE

For me, childhood was a lot of fun and filled with great memories. Home was a safe haven, and family meant love. Having enjoyed an exciting childhood, it is my expectation and desire that my children enjoy their childhood and grow up with great memories. What memories are you leaving your children with?

When I got married, I sincerely desired to be a better parent than my parents. I'd had a great example of parenting with a little insight, but I soon realized that:

- Having the knowledge was different from doing the job.
- My family was different from the family my parents raised.
- The environment in which I was going to raise my children was different from the environment in which I was raised.
- The challenges and opportunities of today are totally different from the challenges and opportunities I had growing up.

While I've realized that every family is different and parenting styles are unique to each family, I have also learned that certain things are basic and can be applied to any situation. You should have a reference point from which you build your own ideals for your family. The scripture is our ultimate reference and standard, but it is also good to learn from people who have applied the standards to the point where they've worked, and from there begin to create your own flair.

I learned so much from my parents, and it is helping me as a parent today. The styles may be different, but the principles remain the same. That is why I am sharing: in the hopes that someone reading this book will be blessed as well. There are virtues you can promote through your parenting, irrespective of your unique parenting style. I learned hard work, integrity, persistence, and contentment. Above all, I learned to love and to put my faith in Christ. These are some of the virtues that I strive to purposefully pass on to my children to build both their faith and their character.

When we had our first child, I began to realize the challenges involved in *purposeful parenting*. Although I had grown up observing my own parents model godly parenting, being a parent, on the other hand, was a different ball game. My husband and I agreed on the kind of family we wanted to build and the kind of lifestyle we wanted to live in order to sustain that family. We wanted our lifestyle to be consistent with the standards of the word of God so as to not unnecessarily expose our children or live a double standard. We desired a simple and realistic lifestyle, and we committed this to God in prayers daily. Even though we knew the purpose we wanted to achieve in our parenting journey, we didn't know the means of getting through, so we began to seek knowledge. I read almost every book I came across that had to do with the subject and began to watch parents who had succeeded or were succeeding at raising godly children in our present generation to see how they were doing it. I asked questions about why they did certain things, and some of them began to mentor me.

As I sought more knowledge on how to maintain the standards of God's word in my parenting, I began to discover not only my true identity as a parent but also, who God has called me to be and the purpose my parenting is meant to accomplish for His glory. I realized that *I have been called to be a destiny helper and a nurturer to my children*, to help guide them through the purpose of God for their lives and to help them understand who they are in order to fulfill God's purpose for their lives.

2

PARENTING FROM MY PERSPECTIVE

*Parents need to fill a child's bucket of self-esteem so high that
the rest of the world can't poke enough holes to drain it dry.*

—ALVIN PRICE

PARENTING MEANS DIFFERENT things to different people, depending on their perception. There are over 1,001 definitions out there, but based on my experience so far on the journey, I have come to agree with the definition that says that: "Parenting is the process of nurturing a child; promoting and supporting the physical, emotional, social, and intellectual development of a child from infancy to adulthood."[1] This refers to the activity of raising a child, not just the biological relationship. I also found this definition to be consistent with Jesus' example in Luke 2:52, which we will explore throughout this book: *"And Jesus increased in wisdom and stature, and in favor with God and men."*

---

1 Martin Davies, *The Blackwell Encyclopedia of Social Work* (Malden: Wiley, 2000), p.245

As a parent, God has called you to nurture your children and to purposefully promote and support their total upbringing: intellectual, physical, spiritual, and social. The scripture admonishes thus: *"But bring them up in the training and admonition of the Lord"* (Ephesians 6:4). To "bring up" in the context of the scripture above means "to nurture, nourish, or provide for with care that nourishes, feeds, or trains." In other words, you are to provide the kind of care that will promote healthy growth and development in all areas of their lives.

Lush and Vredevelt in their book *Mothers and Sons* have likened parenting to a puzzle with many pieces that must be carefully put together to make a meaningful impression.[2] The design of your puzzle and the pieces that come with it will be unique to your family. Therefore, the question is: how do you design your unique parenting puzzle? What are those pieces that must be put together? How do you fit these pieces together to make a meaningful impression? The answers to these questions are unique to each parent. Just like there are usually alternative routes to a destination, there is no conclusive method of parenting. While we don't want a "one size fits all" approach to parenting, there are certain key concepts that we can adopt. The parenting puzzle pieces can be put together through the concept of nurture.

NURTURE

We defined parenting earlier as the process of nurturing a child. *Nurture,* on the other hand, refers to "promoting and supporting the physical, emotional, social, spiritual, and intellectual development of a child from infancy to adulthood." It is the act of providing the right kind of care and attention, and applying God's standards. In order to nurture effectively, it is important that:

---

2 Jean Lush and Pamela Vrendevelt, *Mothers and Sons: Raising Boys to Be Men* (Grand Rapids: Rivell, 1988)

- You understand and deal with each of your children as the unique individuals they are.
- You understand the uniqueness of your child, you prayerfully observe, study, and recognize the individual characteristics of each child and train him or her accordingly.

Every child needs to be dealt with as a unique individual, and nothing should be taken for granted. Take special note and pay particular attention to what is happening in each child's life: responses, weaknesses, habits, attitudes, and so on. Raising children in the same environment does not necessarily mean that all the children will respond in the same way. The blanket approach has been proven to *not work* in most parenting cases. For example, if you have more than one child, you can see how differently each child responds to the family's circumstances. The children are raised under the same roof, fed the same foods in most cases, exposed to the same environment, yet each child responds differently.

Consider the following examples from the Bible: Cain and Abel (Genesis 4) and Jacob and Esau (Genesis 25). Although these siblings were raised in the same environment, they turned out quite differently. This further emphasizes the need for parents to realize the uniqueness of every child and take into consideration their individuality in order to apply purpose to parenting.

THE EFFECT OF NURTURING: SELF-ESTEEM

One great positive effect that comes from proper nurturing of a child is increased self-esteem. Nurturing your child builds positive self-esteem. I grew up believing in myself and in my abilities because my parents made me believe I was the best. They taught me that I had the capacity to be whatever I wanted to be, so they had high expectations of me. Each time I met their expectations, the bar was raised even higher because they believed there was always room for improvement. Soon I realized that I had great potential and all it would take to be the best I could be.

This increased my perception of myself. I couldn't be bothered about how others saw me or what people thought about me as long as I did what was right. What was important to me was how I saw myself through God's eyes.

Self-esteem is the way you feel about yourself and your abilities. It includes self-confidence, self-respect, and self-reliance. It is the collection of beliefs that you have about yourself and can be positive or negative. Hence, we say a person either has a high/positive self-esteem or a low/negative self-esteem. In general, the more positive your self-esteem, the more successful you will be at dealing with life. The same holds for children. The more positive their self-esteem, the more confident and proud they will be of themselves. They will try harder, be happier, and have greater self-respect. Children develop their self-esteem quite early in life. That is why the nurturing of a child starts from the womb. Nurture should be a way of life for every parent.

A healthy self-esteem is your child's armor against challenges in life. Children who feel good about themselves seem to have an easier time handling conflicts and resisting negative pressures. In contrast, for children who have low self-esteem, challenges can become sources of major anxiety and frustration. When children think poorly of themselves, they often have a hard time finding solutions to problems. If children burden themselves with self-critical thoughts like "I don't look good," "My friends will laugh at me," "I can't do anything right," "I know I can't do it," "I know I will fail," "I wish I were someone else," or "I'm no good," they may become passive and withdrawn. Low or negative self-esteem is related to low self-confidence, insecurity, and underachievement.

As a parent or teacher, you have a great influence on the self-esteem of your child or student. For the first four to five years of a child's life, parents are the most important contributors to the life of that child. When the child goes to preschool, caregivers, teachers, and peers become influential in his life. Once he reaches adolescence, peer groups begin to play a greater role in steering the self-esteem of the child. The more positive a child's self-esteem was before adolescence, the easier it will be for him to resist negative peer group pressures. It is part of your role as a parent to foster healthy self-esteem in your child. In fact, you play the major role.

NURTURING A POSITIVE SELF-ESTEEM

No matter what children do or how much you try to protect your children, they will often come across situations that will shake their values and confidence, luring them to compromise. They will encounter peers, especially at school, who will not agree with their values and ideals but will still try to influence them. They will often meet bullies who will want to intimidate them to become who they are not.

I remember enrolling our children in a school outside our home country. My husband had been transferred overseas, on his job and we had to relocate to an environment where we were conspicuously different from the people and racism was quite apparent. We wanted a school where the fear of God and the love of Christ would at least shine bright and perhaps be stronger than differences in skin color. For this reason, we chose this faith-based school and also because it met the educational standards we wanted for our children. However, in that school, our children had the worst racist experiences imaginable, and their self-esteem was greatly shaken as a result. They went through difficult times; they were misunderstood, called names, and looked down upon. They entered the school with strong self-confidence, which posed a problem for some of the people who preferred that our children kept their heads down. By the grace of God, they had the capacity to handle every insult that came their way. They often stood up for themselves, finding ways to confront their bullies without physical contact. However, in the end we had to make a drastic decision to help them maintain their confidence, as there is only so much a person can take (and more so for children). We decided to pull them out of that school, which gave me the opportunity to home school them for two years in order to give them some stability, since we had moved around quite a bit and had to change their school each time.

Children go through difficult times; they need a lot of inner strength to cope with the numerous situations in which they find themselves. To nurture your children's self-esteem, you need to protect them from external influences that affect their perception of themselves and their confidence.

CHILDREN'S REACTION TO CHANGE

Let me digress here and briefly address the issue of change with children. Change tends to put a lot of pressure on children, and they react differently to it. As we nurture our children, it is important that we take note of the different changes that occur in their lives. These could be changes due to relocation, a change of school, physical changes, or whatever it may be. We should be purposeful in helping them through the changes they encounter both in their bodies and in their environment.

My family went through multiple relocations, both internationally and locally, and I found each move to cause a lot of anxiety for our children. Each of these relocations necessitated a change of school, friends, environment, weather, and more. At the same time, these external changes were combined with the emotional and physical changes that were going on in their bodies at various developmental stages. As part of effective nurturing, you should understand the feelings of your child in order to be able to help. It is easy to want to see things flow normally, as if no change has occurred, but you should be sensitive to the need of the child so as to provide the necessary support each time.

TIPS TO EFFECTIVELY NURTURE YOUR CHILDREN

1) CREATE A SAFE, NURTURING HOME ENVIRONMENT
A child who does not feel safe at home or who is being abused at home will suffer immensely from low self-esteem and will not be protected

outside either. Often in the part of the world I come from, parents assume that child abuse, especially sexual abuse and molestation of children, does not exist. Abuse of children exists in various forms: physical, emotional, verbal, psychological, and sexual.

- **Physical Abuse:** This is an assault on a child's body. Experts have defined physical child abuse as any non-accidental injury resulting from beating, hitting, or anything that harms a child's body. This is when a child has been beaten to the point of sustaining injuries on the body, which often happens when parents or other adults act in anger toward a child, often in a bid to discipline the child. This is not discipline, and a child who constantly lives under this condition is being exposed to a lot of danger.
- **Emotional/Psychological Abuse:** This is an assault on a child's psyche. Emotionally abused children often grow up thinking that something is wrong with them, and this affects their self-perception and confidence. It refers to any pattern of behavior toward a child that affects the emotional or social development of that child, including:
  - *Ignoring or rejecting a child:* When the parent or caregiver does not pay any attention to the child or refuses to pay attention to the needs of the child.
  - *Isolating a child:* When parents or caregiver consistently prevent a child from enjoying normal age-appropriate interaction with peers. Such a child is often locked up at home and is not allowed freedom of movement or interaction.
  - *Assaulting a child verbally:* When a child is constantly abused with words: constantly belittled, talked down on, ridiculed, or threatened verbally. Parents in anger call their children such names as "idiot," "stupid," "senseless," "clumsy," "good for nothing," etc., which often causes children to see themselves in such light. This affects the psychology of the child.

- **Sexual Abuse:** Child sexual abuse or molestation is when an adult or adolescent engages a child in any form of sexual activity. Child sexual abuse does not have to involve body contact. When a child is exposed to sexual situations such as pornography and sexually stimulating words, an abuse has occurred. Contrary to the myth still in Africa that only girls can be abused sexually, boys are also in danger of sexual abuse. If more children had caring and nurturing adults they were able to open up to, you would be surprised at the degree and rate of sexual abuse of children going on today. Even more alarming is the frequency of occurrence in the homes or by people who are very close to the family. It is a known fact now that in many cases it is family or household members (rather than strangers) who abuse children sexually.
- **Neglect:** Child neglect is a form of abuse where parents or caregivers do not pay attention to the needs of the child. It is a form of emotional abuse, but I have grouped it differently because oftentimes parents neglect their children without even realizing it. Society will often look at busy parents, who work long hours, as neglecting their children, but the irony is that a parent can be home twenty-four hours of the day with a child and still not pay attention to that child. When you are at home and are not able to connect with your child emotionally, when you are physically around but too busy doing many things and are not available to your child, you are neglecting that child. No parent plans to neglect a child, but being present requires you to make a conscious effort to meet the needs of your child, whether or not you are physically available.

As purposeful parents, you must make your homes safe for your children by eliminating anything that will expose your family to danger. Watch out for signs of abuse by others, especially domestic workers and relatives who are in your home. Also watch out for problems in school, trouble with peers, and other factors that may affect your child's self-esteem. Deal with these issues very sensitively and swiftly. Not handling such issues properly might further expose your child.

2) BE NATURAL AND WARM WITH YOUR CHILD

Your love will go a long way in boosting your child's self-esteem. When a child is pressured outside, she needs to be reassured in the loving arms of her parents. She can endure situations outside knowing that she will always get comfort from the warm embrace of her parents.

Children love affirmation, and one of the quickest ways to build a child's self-esteem is through "honest praise." Children should be showered with realistic praise when they have done well. Make sure the praise is realistic and honest. Don't be the kind of parent who only notices when your children do something wrong; it is also important that you look out for when they do things right and then commend them for that. There is a hero in every child. Focus on the positive behavior of your child, while you lovingly correct any misbehavior. Celebrate and develop your child's multiple gifts and talents.

3) IDENTIFY AND REDIRECT YOUR CHILD'S INACCURATE BELIEFS

It is very important for parents to identify their children's irrational beliefs about themselves, whether about perfection, attractiveness, ability, or anything else. Helping your child set more accurate standards and be more realistic in self-evaluation will ensure that he has a healthier self-awareness. Inaccurate perceptions of self can take root and become reality to your child. For example, a child who does very well academically in school but has issues with one subject like mathematics may say, "I am a terrible student." Not only is this a false generalization, it's also a belief that will set him up for failure. Encourage your child to see the situation in its true light. Remind your child of all the other subjects he excels in, while continuing to seek ways to raise your child's achievement/attainment in the difficult subject.

I must say here that this is not an excuse for failure or mediocrity. I do have high expectations of my own children. They are expected to do well in all their subjects to the best of their varying abilities, considering their strengths and weaknesses. Our job as parents is to continue to encourage their strengths and find ways to help them improve in the areas they appear weak in.

Be realistic in your expectations of your child; watch your words and actions. Children are very sensitive to their parents' words. Remember to praise a child, not only for a job well done, but also for the effort invested. For example, if your child takes part in a school competition and does not come out the winner, don't ignore the fact that she was bold enough to make an attempt. Consider the amount of effort your child put into making it to that stage, and rather say something like "Well, you didn't make it this time, but I am really proud of the effort you put into it." Do not reward outcomes alone; also reward effort and completion.

4) AVOID COMPARISON

It is counterproductive to compare your child with other children or with siblings, although it is good to encourage your child to emulate good behavior. Try to catch your child doing what is right, and acknowledge it. When it becomes a habit to always refer to what some other child did well (where your child did not do as well) in a way that the child's self-esteem is trampled on, you are simply telling that child that he can never do anything right. That is emotional/psychological abuse, and a child who constantly gets such a message will live to believe that he is not good enough, which will definitely impact his self-esteem.

As parents, we should always keep in mind that children are different in every way. No two children, including twins, are exactly the same. Every child has areas in which she is talented and excels. Therefore, you must see each child as a unique individual. There is a hero in every child.

5) BE A POSITIVE ROLE MODEL

If you are excessively harsh on yourself or pessimistic or unrealistic about your abilities and limitations, your child may eventually mirror you. It is important and ultimately to your child's advantage that you nurture your own self-esteem as well, so that your child can have a great role model.

6) AVOID ACTIONS THAT MAY LOWER YOUR CHILD'S SELF-ESTEEM

- Do not expect too much or too little from your child. Children have the capacity to take in whatever you expose them to. Create the right exposure and opportunity for your child to thrive.
- Do not criticize children in front of others. When you make the child an object of ridicule, you are trampling on his self-esteem and exposing him to the ridicule of others.
- Do not use curse words or call your child "stupid," "idiot," "thoughtless," or "clumsy." Understand that the words you speak over your child are prophecies. Yes, children may behave silly, lazy, or clumsy sometimes, but that is not who they are. You must speak positively into your child's life.
- Often praise and show your child appreciation; Children do better when they are praised and appreciated for the things they did right, especially by their parents. Just knowing that their parents believe in them motivates them to do even better.
- Do not call children failures, even when they have made mistakes. Remember, *"Death and life are in the power of the tongue"* (Proverbs 18:21). Only confess what you want for your child, and speak purpose into the life of your child.
- Do not overprotect or neglect your children. There is a thin line here. Some parents tend to overprotect their children, not giving them room to express themselves and flourish, while some completely neglect their children in the bid to provide for them. We should learn to create a balance and provide nurture through our unconditional love. Children thrive in a balanced environment. Give them the opportunity to do what they can do for themselves; it gives them a sense of self-worth and accomplishment.

I must emphasize at this point that there is no conclusive way to nurture a child. The points outlined here are guidelines that are working for me and I believe are worth sharing. By its very nature, nurturing is a creative and deliberate activity that can take many forms. Any activity you engage in that shows your children they are loved without compromising standards will be an effective act of nurturing.

3

WHAT KIND OF PARENT ARE YOU?

To bring up a child in the way that he should go, travel that way yourself.

—JOSH BILLINGS

A S YOU STRIVE to nurture and raise your children, bear in mind that God has His divine purpose for every child and that should be the purpose that you ultimately strive to achieve. God's purpose for your child goes beyond becoming a doctor, engineer, or lawyer. God has a plan for every child, which is way beyond whatever we hope they become in the future: that they are brought up in the nurture and admonition of the Lord.

From the example of Jesus in his early life on Earth, according to our theme scripture in Luke 2:52, which bears repetition *("And Jesus increased in wisdom and stature, and in favor with God and men"),* and from our definition of parenting (the process of promoting a child's intellectual, physical, spiritual, and social development). God's purpose for our parenting is to help our children develop like Christ did: in wisdom (intellectually), in stature (physically), in favor with God (spiritually), and in favor with humans (socially). God wants us to raise "total children," children who are sound in every area of their lives, including their spiritual lives.

PASSIVE VERSUS PURPOSEFUL PARENTING

Some parents today take a *"passive* approach to parenting rather than a *purposeful* mind-set. They desire that their children follow directions, respect authority, and grow into responsible adults, but their responses to typical childhood issues reflect the opposite. If you seek to fulfill purpose in your parenting assignment, then passivity is not an option.

PASSIVE PARENTING

Passivity is the enemy to effective parenting and an enemy to your child's destiny. Many parents are good churchgoing people, loyal employees in their workplaces, and successful businessmen and women, and yet are passive or inactive on the home front. Passive parenting is dangerous to your child's well-being, and as a parent, you cannot afford to be neither hot nor cold in the affairs of your children.

The story of Eli in the Bible (1 Samuel 2:12–36) is a story of passive parenting. Eli was a priest: that is, the modern-day pastor, or like a lot of Christian parents today who are actively committed to the work of God (the dad who is a dedicated usher or committed minister, or the mum who is a faithful Sunday school teacher). Eli had two sons the Bible describes as "wicked men who had no regard for the Lord." These young men were stealing from the Jews who gave their sacrifices to God and sleeping with the women who served at the Tent of Meeting. We read in the scriptures that their sin was "very great in the Lord's sight." And yet Eli, their father, the priest, was passive. He did nothing to stop them from their evil act. Rather, he posed the passive parenting question of some parents today: "Why do you do such things? I hear from all the people about these wicked deeds of yours." Doesn't this sound familiar: "Why do you want to break my heart?" or "Do you want me to die?" or "Do you want your daddy to be angry and stop paying your school fees?" Eli relied on the reports of others rather than being purposeful in his duties as a father. He was vibrant in the things of God but kept his parental head in the sand. Of course, as we read in the scriptures, God rebuked him for his passivity in raising his children with the purpose God intended.

Passive parents empower their children to go astray. And in that way, the parents participate in the child's sin and dishonor God. You can see that Eli was punished for the sins his children committed because he failed to take his position as the father and do what he was supposed to do. He was passive! Some parents today, even in the midst of their passiveness, believe they are doing all they should do, often in ignorance of what they should be doing or simply with the "It doesn't matter" attitude. Passive parents have an obvious look: they are the ones who turn the other way when their child is misbehaving, and they rationalize their child's behavior.

Passive parents are those who are unaware of the influences in their child's life through media, peer pressure, and other sources. They often do not place healthy boundaries around their children and allow them to explore life beyond what their emotional and spiritual maturity can handle. Passive parents are those who allow and expect others to raise their children for them, "outsourcing" parenting to nannies and caregivers. They get other people to do the job they are supposed to be doing and pay whatever it will cost them. This is passivity. There is nothing wrong with getting "help" when it is needed, but you should not be delegating your core responsibility as a parent.

As a Sunday school teacher, I've had the experience where a parent blamed her child's inability to reflect the word of God on Sunday school teachers who are with the children for only about three hours a week. I have also seen parents in the secular schools blame teachers for their children not attaining their desired success. The truth is this: God is not going to hold those teachers solely accountable for your child, because they are just a small part of the total upbringing of your child. As a parent, you have the major responsibility to raise your children right, and you must take that responsibility seriously. On the other hand, if you are a teacher (in Sunday school, in a secular school, or even a lesson teacher) reading this and thinking you are exonerated, you should understand that God will have you account for the part you play in the life of every child in your care for that period of time.

Obviously, you can see that passivity is an enemy to your child's future. If we remain passive in our parenting duties, no matter what excuses we may have, we will be mortgaging the future of our children, and another generation will be lost. What, then, does it mean to be *purposeful* in parenting?

PURPOSEFUL PARENTING

Purposeful parents are those who are mindful of the relationship between the present and the future. They understand that what is currently happening in their child's life affects his future. As a matter of fact, the first thirteen years of a child's life will shape the remainder of that life. Purposeful parents are those who understand the truth that they can change their world with the children God gave them. When a parent is purposeful, he or she takes time to sit down and ask these questions:

- What character traits do I hope my child has when he becomes an adult?
- How should she see God and herself when she grows up?
- How do I want my child to relate to friends, spouse, and his own children when he becomes an adult?

These and other questions define the outcome you are seeking. If you want selfish and immature adult children, then be passive and you will reach your goals. If, on the other hand, you desire your children to be mature, responsible, generous adults, it begins today with *purposeful parenting.*

My husband and I are blessed with three children (a son and two daughters). Our utmost desire for them is that they become people of integrity, willing to work hard; those who value people more than things; and adults who are passionately in love with God. It is our desire *"that our son may be like a plant grown up in its youth and our daughters may be as pillars sculptured in palace style"* (Psalms 144:12), with so much inner beauty.

These goals have monumental implications in our day-to-day parenting; they bring direction to where we are going and set the course of our parenting journey. We are determined to pass on the legacy our parents passed down to us. I am a third-generation Christian in my family, and this legacy has been passed down all the way from my grandmother. My husband also had his father pass on to him the legacy of Christ. Our desire is to also give our children the legacy of "Christ and education," bringing them up in the nurture and admonition of the Lord. As my dad once explained to me, "Christ is the most important personality they need in their lives to succeed, and education will open doors to the opportunities they need to succeed in life."

Ultimately, *purposeful parenting* is more strategic than tactical. Purposeful parents are thinking more about the effects on the future instead of what feels good at the moment. The strategic parent or purposeful parent knows: *"While the earth remains, seedtime and harvest, cold and heat, winter and summer, day and night shall not cease"* (Genesis 8:22). What they put into their children today is exactly what they will get back when the harvest is ripe. Purposeful parenting, however, does not happen without sacrifice, and passive parenting has its own sacrifices, too. It is one or the other. If you are not sacrificing *for your child*, then you will be sacrificing *your child.* Sacrifice in this context means giving up your comfort, sometimes for the long-term spiritual and emotional health of your family.

Purposeful parenting also means being really involved in your children's lives—knowing what they are up to and setting some positive *boundaries* to guide their behavior and decisions. The first twelve to thirteen years of your child's life is the classroom where they will learn the answers to many questions. This is when their view of God (their biblical world view) will be established, their self-worth will be infused, their view of relationships will be learned, and their character will be grounded. That is how important your role is as a parent. Purposeful parents recognize this and live in the present with an eye to the future.

4

EDUCATION AS A DOOR TO YOUR CHILD'S FUTURE

Education is a better safeguard of liberty than a standing army.

—EDWARD EVERETT

ONE OF THE four areas that God expects our children to be nurtured, following the example of Jesus in Luke 2:52, is "in wisdom." This can be interpreted to mean intellectually. Jesus was full of wisdom and understanding. He was brilliant! The scripture tells of how He taught the people in the synagogue and answered all their questions brilliantly. He exposed himself to knowledge, and He knew the word of God. Is it any wonder that He had the right answers when the enemy tempted him?

One general way we develop our children's intellect is by sending them to school to acquire education. Every child has a unique ability, and as I mentioned earlier, children are different and unique in their ability to learn.

THE MIND OF A CHILD

For the first year or two outside the womb, the child is in the most impressionable state she will ever be in. The environment she finds herself in gradually shapes her brain. As a purposeful parent who is strategic, you can have a huge influence on your newborn's first encounters with life and learning. The mind learns optimally when appropriately challenged in an environment that encourages learning. According to *Merriam-Webster,* "Intellect is the power of knowing as distinguished from the power to feel and to will." It is the capacity for knowledge and the capacity for rational or intelligent thought, especially when highly developed.

Various research studies have shown that the early years of a child's life involve the highest rates of learning, and the habits formed at a young age will stay with children for most of their lives.[3] When children are young, it's the perfect time to introduce them to books that educate and inform. Children of any age can benefit from experiencing books on a daily basis, and it's always best to make time for children to read or be read to every day. Books help to develop the imagination of a child and expand his world. Motivation is said to be the key to learning. You can help your child discover this thirst for knowledge before he is even old enough to go to school or to read. Here are tips to help your child attain his intellectual potentials:

1) READ TO YOUR CHILD DAILY.
Fill your home with lots of books/reading material—storybooks, novels, newspapers, and magazines—even if your child cannot read yet.

---

3 "Speaking for Children: The Early Years," First Five Sonoma County. Last modified April 2009. http://www.first5sonomacounty.org/documents/news-letters/english/the_early_years.pdf

Children are influenced by their surroundings. You should cultivate the habit of reading yourself. When a child sees her parent reading, it makes an impression, just like anything she sees you do consistently. As parents, you can foster the love for learning, as you are the most important modeling agents in your child's life.

2) ENCOURAGE YOUR CHILD TO EXPLORE HIS INTERESTS.
If you have a child who loves animals, for instance, offer him some educational books about animals. Allow such a child to explore Animal Planet or the National Geographic Channel, which also helps to make the best of TV time. You could also direct him to websites that explore animal facts. Your enthusiasm over your child's areas of interest is motivation in itself.

3) PROVIDE PLAY OPPORTUNITIES THAT OFFER DIFFERENT TYPES OF LEARNING STYLES.
Play is one of the most powerful vehicles through which children master new skills, concepts, and experiences, which can even help them solve some of the challenges they'll meet later on in school. For example, through play with blocks or jigsaw puzzles, your toddler can develop her creative expression and problem-solving skills.

4) CELEBRATE ACHIEVEMENTS.
Reward your child for large and small achievements, whether it is finishing a book or completing a school project. Positive reinforcement encourages children to continue to challenge themselves. As central role models, parents and guardians have the responsibility to create an environment that fosters a love for learning. It is a known fact that the more children read, the better readers and writers they become.

THE SCHOOL AND LEARNING
School is a major agent of intellectual development for children. However, the school does not have the exclusive job of educating the child and is not meant to be the only agent teaching your child. A lot

is left to parents to ensure their children get a well-rounded education. Parents work in partnership with the school when it comes to educating children. More importantly, children need a lot more knowledge and exposure than what is provided in the classroom to survive in the real world. And it is you as the parent (not just the teacher) who will provide the atmosphere for that well-rounded education.

Children should also be encouraged to explore their environment and make an effort to learn. Foster a desire in your child to seek information. For example, when your child comes to you (as children often do) for the meaning of a new word he has just come across during the course of reading a book, completing assignments, or even after having a conversation with someone, the easiest thing would be for you to go ahead and tell him the meaning of the word. However, it would be more helpful to your child if you referred him to the dictionary or gave clues from the text to help him find the answer. Sometimes your child will discover that the word has more than one meaning. Then you can step in to help him understand the context of discussion and the appropriate meaning. A child going through this process would have learned more than he was seeking to learn initially.

Guiding your child through figuring out solutions for herself helps her to engage her brain and learn to seek knowledge independently. This approach will help children research and discover things by themselves, without waiting for the teacher, and it exposes them to lifelong learning. When children ask questions, they want to know. An eagerness to know what is going on in the world around them is a positive trait and should be encouraged as much as possible. Not only will your child be perceived as being vastly well read and knowledgeable, but she will also be more aware of opportunities out there and will be less likely to miss a good opportunity when it comes along.

THE PARENT/SCHOOL PARTNERSHIP

Not much can be gleaned from the school experience without the active involvement of the parents. I would call it a joint venture. The school cannot work in isolation, and there are many ways parents can help children achieve maximum academic potential.

First and foremost, you must identify the need for quality education for your child. Education is fundamental to the development of any country's future and to the future of every child. High expectations begin right from the start in the home; we should therefore make learning part of our children's daily activities. Giving children an education is not just about sending them to school every day; it calls for some commitment on the part of the parent as well. Parents have to assume the role of teachers sometimes.

What can you do as a parent to contribute to the overall education of your child? Teachers are trained to teach what is outlined in the curriculum, but parents have a major role to play in the upbringing of their children and in discovering and then developing their potentials. Education is much more than just teaching curriculum; it is about giving the child tools to succeed in life—life skills. How do they apply curriculum to life situations? There are many ways you can help achieve this, including working hand in hand with your child's teacher and being part of your child's educational process.

At Home

"The best school of learning is the home."

(Anonymous)

Children's talents should be developed as early as possible so they can achieve their full potential. Parents don't need to be educated themselves—or have a great deal of money or even much time—to be able to help children learn and improve their ability to think and communicate. Here are some tips for helping your children reach their academic potential:

SET HIGH ACADEMIC GOALS FOR YOUR CHILD

Children must be made to understand that success is possible and that they will benefit later in life from working hard and doing well in school. Let them know that their family and teachers expect them to do well. Help them develop a sense of pride in what they do. In his book *Gifted Hands*, Ben Carson tells of how his mother was able to influence his future with positive words and by consistently letting her sons know they were carrying greatness inside of them and should not settle for less. She constantly exposed them to books and lots of reading. Ben, who was once at the very bottom of his class, rose to be one of the most celebrated neurosurgeons in the world today.[4]

Let me mention here that the academic goals you set for your child must be realistic and achievable. It will be unrealistic to set a goal of distinction for a child who obviously has a special education need. That child might never meet that goal. When you set goals, you must take into consideration the ability of your child. Do not compare your child with other children, because every child is different. Your child might not make a distinction the first time, but what you want to see is that she is putting in her best effort and that there is consistent improvement. Perhaps, someday, she will get there.

INTERACT WITH YOUR CHILD

Each evening, have conversations about current events and happenings in the news, and talk about what you all did during the day. As you go through your daily routine, explain what you are doing and why. Encourage your child to ask questions, and make up stories together. Read to him, play games, and solve puzzles together. Pay attention to what your child likes to do; it could be drawing, working with numbers, music, or sports. Help him develop those skills, or find out where in the community he can participate in learning enrichment activities. This strategy creates lasting bonds, providing a platform for open communication between you and your child.

---

4 Ben Carson, *Gifted Hands: The Ben Carson Story* (Grand Rapids: Zondervan, 1990).

I realized that my children enjoyed it a lot whenever we did things together, and they still do. It makes them happy, and I gain a lot of fulfillment when we spend time with them doing what we all enjoy. When we are in a relaxed mood, nobody holds back and we can talk about anything. For example, our son enjoys fixing things with his dad, assembling a new piece of furniture, changing or pumping car tires, washing the car, playing video games, or a trip to the barber shop (which gives them the opportunity to be alone in the car and talk about almost anything). They both usually come back home happy and excited each time they go out together because bonding would have taken place. Dinnertime is also a very special time for us. When we all sit at the table for dinner, it is always an avenue for bonding. That is where we talk about our day and share funny jokes while enjoying our meal.

GETTING INVOLVED

All parents are partners in their children's education, and all parents have a place in their children's school, regardless of their own educational or economic status. The need to get involved in your child's school cannot be overemphasized. Paying attention to little details—things like reading notices and newsletters, and understanding school rules and policies—helps to create a comfortable learning platform for your child.

I remember when our children were in preschool that the children were asked to wear a specific color shirt over jeans on a particular day for a school event. This was an event on the school calendar, which was given out to every parent at the beginning of term. The information appeared in the school's weekly newsletter the week before, and two days prior to the event, reminders were sent home. Again, the day before, teachers wrote reminders in the children's communication books. Then came the main day: children were arriving that morning beautifully dressed in that color and full of excitement. I noticed a little girl who was reluctant to get out of the car, and the nanny who accompanied her was trying to force her out. The child was wearing her regular school uniform, so she felt odd as soon as she got to the school gate and observed that she was about the only one looking different.

When situations like this occur, they create insecurity in children. This child could have been put in this situation just for any reason—the easiest may have been that the parent probably did not read the notices or just didn't pay particular attention. Perhaps the parent did not consider it important and so did not make any effort to get that child a shirt of that color if she didn't already own it. It is even possible that the child had that color of shirt hanging in her wardrobe but nobody reminded her to put it on. Whatever the reason may have been, we must realize the negative effect this kind of carelessness or oversight can have on children.

My admonition here is that we pay attention to the minute details about our children's lives. In balancing this, I would say that there is no perfect parent; we are all mortal beings and are bound to forget or make mistakes. Sometimes we are so busy with other things that are equally as important, especially when both parents work outside the home and usually for long hours. Good organization will help you avoid this kind of oversight. I recommend that mums have a handy calendar where they can note important dates and set reminders if possible. Once I receive the school's calendar, I take the time to set reminders on my phone, which helps to keep me organized. Let's put our smartphones to smart use.

When parents care and become active participants in the educational process, their children benefit enormously. Parents should be knowledgeable about the educational program their child is enrolled in and should be actively involved with the school.

There is so much controversy and confusion out there about the curriculum that different private schools offer. In Nigeria, for example, you hear some schools saying they run the British curriculum and some the American curriculum, and others claim to be mixing all. It will amaze you to know that some of the school administrators themselves are confused and do not even know what they are doing. Some have no direction but are just copying what everyone else is doing and adopting terms that seem to appeal to parents. Make time to seek understanding about the system, curriculum, or learning approach that your child's school has adopted, and understand why and how that will work for your child.

To make your relationship with the school productive, show the staff respect and make them feel important because they really are important to your children's education. Listen to their points of view, show some flexibility, and find compromises whenever possible. Always keep in mind that both you and the school have the same goal in mind; and the goal is to educate your child. Active involvement in the parent-teacher association (PTA) or whatever parents' forum is available at your child's school is an excellent way to provide the school with help and input in an organized manner.

Another way you can get involved and be supportive of your child's education is by having the right attitude toward school functions and activities. This way you can help make school exciting and fun for your child. During school functions and events, especially if the child is playing a special role, you are the fan your child wants to see. Encouraging children to participate in social events at school is of great value, and you will notice that once they get on stage, the first person they want to see is you (their mum or dad) and they will begin to look out for you in the audience. It is appropriate for you to help them locate where you are. Once your child identifies you in the audience, you will see the smile on his face and then an increase in confidence, as he knows you are there for him. You are the most important audience to your child at that time.

Always let your child know how wonderful she was on stage. No matter what the performance actually looked like, even if she could have done better, always be conscious to not bring down your child's morale. Find something she did well and focus on it, and also find a good way to correct her mistakes to help her perform better next time.

Parents often expect their children to come out winners each and every time they participate in competitions, but you and I know that it doesn't turn out that way all the time in the real world. So while we help our children to develop the good habit of hard work and always putting forth their best in any task that they are given, we need to learn to reward efforts and not just outcomes. Encouragement helps to bring out the best in children, and you are in the best position as parents to provide this encouragement for your child.

PURPOSEFUL RELATIONSHIP WITH YOUR CHILD'S TEACHER

When talking about the intellectual development of the child and the school being a key player in this, it's important to mention that our involvement, encouragement, and support to our children and the teacher is pivotal to getting the desired outcome in our children. The following key points should be followed if learning is to be a pleasant experience for your child.

DEVELOP A POSITIVE PARENT/TEACHER RELATIONSHIP

It's important to establish a good and cordial relationship with your child's teacher. Be open and supportive each time you meet with your child's teacher, and always strive for cooperation. Even when the teacher describes a negative side of your child's behavior or informs you of other problems, try to remain objective. If you and the teacher are unable to work together to solve the problem, you can end up exposing your child to more serious difficulties. You can ensure the teacher moves beyond simply pointing out problems by also suggesting possible solutions.

You may ask, "How do I remain objective (even when my child's inadequacies are being highlighted) and maintain a good balance?" I have learned to step into the shoes of the teacher, which helps me move into a neutral position. In other words, if it weren't my child, would it have been OK? Encourage your child's teacher to suggest ideas for eliminating or reducing the problem where possible. If an immediate suggestion cannot be provided, then a follow-up is necessary. You and your child's teacher must work together. It's also important to let the teacher know the measures you are taking at home so he or she can follow up on that for consistency. On the other hand, even when your child is doing well, it is also helpful to find out what you can do to ensure continued success and progress. Discuss ways to increase your child's growth, because no matter how well your child is doing, there is a need to sustain the progress and room for continuous growth.

While seeking to establish a good relationship with your child's teacher, you should also be sensitive to your parental instinct. I had an experience where I was doing everything possible to cooperate with my child's teacher; it looked like we were working together, but little did I know that the teacher was not genuine. Each time my child came home, she would report experiences she was having with the teacher that were contrary to what I had perceived of the teacher from my interactions with her. That was a case of "a wolf in sheep's clothing." With a teacher like this, you have to be careful and tactically work along with her. Communicate with her more by e-mail as a way of documenting your discussions, especially on sensitive issues.

MAKE THE FIRST MEETING WITH YOUR CHILD'S TEACHER PLEASANT

The first contact with your child's teacher is extremely important in numerous ways. This is the time both you and the teacher create a first impression of each other, build rapport, and develop a relationship of trust. Therefore, it is important to commit this first meeting to God in prayers. Pray for sensitivity, discernment, and favor. A good time to meet with your child's teacher is during the "meet the teacher" meeting (or whatever your school calls it) just before school starts. It is important that parents endeavor to be at this first meeting. If for some unavoidable reason you are unable to be there, you should make sure you get to meet your child's teacher during the first week of school. This gives you and the teacher the opportunity to meet each other when neither of you have any complaints. If you miss the opportunity to meet your teacher in his or her "most pleasant" moment, the first teacher contact could be very unpleasant. The teacher is usually calling to discuss the child's progress, which may not be a pleasant discussion, or to report some unacceptable behavior or concern about the progress of your child. This kind of contact puts the parent on the defensive and may hamper communication. In this case, neither party wins, with the biggest loser usually being the child.

During the first week of school, the teacher probably knows very little about your child. Therefore, it is your responsibility to provide helpful information about your child and also to assure the teacher that he or she has your full support and cooperation. The most effective way to get the best out of your child in school is to work with the teacher. If you both work in isolation, a loophole will be created. Provide the teacher with your phone number, and let him or her know that he or she is free to call when help is required from home. This always proves to be effective. Your child's teacher should know from the beginning that you want to work with him or her. This is the greatest expectation every good teacher has of parents, because when parents work hand in hand with teachers, it makes the job of the teacher a lot easier, as it creates room for consistency and eliminates double standards. Then the child has even more to gain.

It's important you have an open mind when you are meeting your child's teacher for the first time. Sometimes parents come in with impressions based on what they may have heard from other parents or students about a teacher without understanding the circumstances behind such stories. Always be optimistic when your child is moving to a new class. This will come much easier if you have taken time to pray in advance for the next teacher your child will have.

With regards to prayer, let me mention here that there is nothing too small to take to God in prayer, and God indeed answers prayers. I have found it very rewarding to commit my children's teachers to God ahead of time. Each time the children are moving to a new class, I take time to pray during the holidays about their teachers and classmates—that God will give them teachers that will help fulfill God's purpose in their lives that year. It's also important to pray for a teacher who can accommodate the personality of your child. Once a teacher who had been assigned to teach one of my children resigned before school started and another teacher had to be reassigned to the class. I cannot say for sure why that happened, but one thing I know is that it was all in God's plan and in favor of my child. It was obvious that we couldn't have had a better teacher than we had that year. Some people have argued that it doesn't really matter, since in many cases, teachers remain in their classes. For example, a year four teacher will most likely teach year four the following year, and it is almost always obvious who the next teacher will be. This is more often than not true according to the plan of humans, but I have seen and experienced God move things around in our favor and for our good. I will dwell more on prayer in a subsequent chapter.

Some parents stay away from their child's school and only show up when the school summons them. When you get involved, you are indicating to the school that you are truly concerned that your child receives good education. Sometimes parents with low levels of education get intimidated and do not think they have anything to offer. Like I stated earlier, your level of education does not matter as long as you know what you want for your child—as long as you have a purpose and are able to pursue it. You have a place in your child's school regardless of your educational background or social status. However, learning occurs every day throughout life, and so improving yourself daily will help you become more aware and more comfortable. The scripture says, *"A man of knowledge increases power"* (Proverbs 24:5b). Irrespective of your level of education, you need to understand the school system and how things work. Be well informed about what is happening in the system. It is not enough to know that the "educational system is bad"; it is much more important to know the current issues that face education and the efforts your child's school is making to handle such issues.

Consistency is key. Being consistent in your interaction with the teacher or the school will help you track your child's progress so you can easily tell, even without being told, when the child is having a problem. Again, if both parents work long hours and are hardly available physically, you might consider calling in every once in a while and sending notes to the teacher frequently to check on your child's progress. The secret remains that once the teacher realizes your child's education is important to you and you are involved, he or she will always be ready to work with you and sometimes even go the extra mile. On the other hand, if you give the teacher the impression that you are not interested, it is easy for him or her to overlook little details about your child, which could in turn create serious problems.

However, it is important to understand that the teacher's teaching time is the children's time and should be respected. Be sensitive to that, and do not demand the teacher's time unnecessarily. It is advisable to work within the teacher's time frame and not just show up when you like and expect the teacher to leave the children to attend to you. Try not to be in the teacher's face all the time; e-mail or text messages will allow the teacher to respond to you during her noncontact time.

ENSURE A PRODUCTIVE RELATIONSHIP

Be careful to ensure that your relationship with the school and/or with your child's teacher is mutual and always productive. Some parents, rather than sincerely seeking the good for their child and the school, are more interested in complaining and creating problems in the school. This kind of attitude will always be to your child's disadvantage. Your goal should always be to make a positive impact.

Every school has its peculiar issues. I personally do not believe that there is a perfect school anywhere. The good schools are those that continue to strive for excellence, consistently improving their program offerings and delivery. While schools try their best to provide enabling learning environments and quality educational programs, every school has one issue or another it has to deal with. Your job is to prayerfully determine which school environment and program will best meet the educational, social, and spiritual needs of your child. (You may not achieve everything to the fullest from one school, but it is important to weigh your options prayerfully.) Once you've been able to identify the school that will work best for your children, give them all the support you can and make a positive impact in the school.

FIRST ENCOUNTER

With our family's multiple relocations, one of the decisions we had to make each time was what school would be best for our children. This was always a major decision for us. One time it was in the middle of the school year, and we had to quickly get our children into a school. Our first and second oldest children were little over four and six years old at the time. After visiting a couple of schools, we finally made a decision.

We enrolled them in Nursery 2 and Primary 2 respectively. On their first day of school, I dropped them off without getting an opportunity to meet with their teachers. Since it was the middle of the school year, we had not attended the "meet the teacher" meeting at the beginning of the year. I couldn't have a chat with their teachers that morning, as it would mean encroaching into the teaching time. So I planned to see and familiarize myself with the teachers when I picked the children up at the end of the school day.

I made my way to my son's classroom at the close of school the same day with the purpose of meeting his teacher. When I walked into the room, the teacher walked up to me and I introduced myself. Almost immediately, she said, "Madam, we have been trying to reach you." She told me that my son could not do anything they did in class that day. That morning, they did a bit of review on what the class had learned previously, and she had asked him a few questions, which he did not answer. She had something written on the whiteboard that she asked him to read, and he wouldn't do this either. Instead, he kept gazing at the playground (which he could view through his classroom window) and clearly wanted to go out to play. So the teacher had concluded that he wasn't right for that class, which meant moving him back.

I asked her if that was all, and she said yes, so I laughed. I laughed because I knew my child, and I knew exactly what he was up to. She went further to say that he could not even pronounce his name clearly, and neither was he able to write it (you know how one thing always leads to another). I was very calm because I knew exactly what was going on, and I knew my son was capable of doing everything the teacher had asked him to do. So I requested a sheet of paper, which I gave to him along with a pencil, and I asked him to write his name. He wrote his first and surname in full, capitalizing the first letters. Then I asked him to pronounce the name to the teacher, and he did, very clearly. Then I went further by asking him to read out loud what had been written on the whiteboard; they were words he knew already, and so he read each word out very clearly. The teacher was amazed.

I quickly used that opportunity to have my first meeting with her. I explained to her that my child was intelligent and smart, but playful, too. I explained that he was only playing on her intelligence; he wanted to see if the teacher would let him have his way because he'd just moved from a system where children, especially that young didn't have to do anything they didn't want to do. I also let her know that if she was firm and consistent with him, she would soon realize the quality of pupil she had. We exchanged ideas on how she could work with him using positive reinforcement. I made her understand that she had my full support and cooperation, and went on to tell her a few relevant things about my son. At the end of the meeting, she said to me, "Madam, don't worry. Now I get it, and I know what to do."

I was able to turn that first unexpected and possibly unpleasant meeting into a productive one, which helped me to develop a good relationship with the teacher. My son did exceptionally well in that class, and the teacher became one of the best teachers we ever had. Even after he left that class and the school, I have maintained a very positive relationship with that wonderful teacher.

UNDERSTAND THE DO'S AND DON'TS

During the first week of school, many teachers explain their expectations for the child's work and classroom behavior, as well as the consequences of not complying with these rules. Some schools will give a school handbook to parents/students that contains all the policies and expectations of the school. Ensure that your child understands the guidelines early. By doing this, you can help her get off to a good start in the class. Most classroom teachers have established reasonable expectations and boundaries. Parents should make sure their children know what the acceptable and non-acceptable behaviors are. We must help our children understand that rules are there to guide them and not to harm them, and that once they abide by the school's rules, they are not likely to get into trouble.

Do not make the mistake of giving your child the impression that the teacher's expectations are not to be taken seriously, as I have seen some parents do. If you do so, you will be setting that child up for failure because he will never take anything the teacher says seriously, and this is wrong. If you have issues with the teacher's expectations, find time to discuss this objectively with the teacher, but always make sure your child obeys the rules set for the class.

HOMEWORK

One of the most important assets a child can have is a parent who is involved in her education. Some parents see homework as a burden, while others demonstrate a positive attitude toward it. I have discovered with my children that homework helps to reinforce what they have learned in school. A lot of children do not have the discipline to pick up their books ordinarily to study, but with homework they do not have a choice (although homework should not take the place of studying). Usually children need more of motivation than actual assistance to get the homework done. Sometimes they really might not have understood a concept well when they were taught in class. Therefore, your support can be very helpful.

I have heard parents say something like: "The teachers are being paid to do the work. Why should they send the work home?" Especially when their children attend private schools, some parents feel they have paid for the job to be done, and this includes the homework. Make it a routine to always go through your child's work to see what he has done and what he is expected to do, and help where you can and should. Your involvement shouldn't be helping the child to do the work but letting him do the work by himself with your supervision and assistance where necessary. Creating a conducive studying and learning environment around the house will also help.

There is a tendency for parents to be overwhelmed sometimes with the level of work the children bring home these days. I once heard about a mother who coped well enough with supervising and assisting her children in their homework at the elementary level. However, as they went higher, she couldn't cope anymore because she felt she didn't know so much, especially with mathematics. She had to enroll herself in a math class at a community college just to be able to help her children. That is how passionate and purposeful one parent decided to be. It may sound ridiculous, but that parent sure had purpose in mind. We have to keep learning. However, where the parent's level of literacy cannot carry it, it might be necessary to hire the support of a private tutor (home lesson teacher). In my own experience, I have learned a lot of things I didn't know before and have been reminded of some that I knew but had forgotten just by supervising my children's homework.

I remember attending a job interview for an administrative position in a school, and the first test I had to take was a written English test. When I looked through the questions, they were the kind of English questions my elementary children brought home as homework. They were simple plural nouns and simple past tense, but they were the kind of tenses one would often overlook in spoken English. I must confess that I was able to excel on that test because I had been working with my children on similar topics, unaware that I was also preparing myself for a test. So when we supervise our children's homework, this is also an avenue for us to keep learning and keep our memories refreshed on subjects taught in school. We should be lifelong learners.

STUDY AND HOMEWORK PRACTICES

Certain key practices make life easier for the entire family when it comes to study time and organization. Children need to be able to concentrate to do their work and do it well. Here are some important home practices to consider implementing:

- Take away any form of distraction. Ensure that television sets are turned off during study or homework time. Leaving the TV set on will always draw children's attention away from their work.
- Designate a specific area in the house for homework or studying when possible; it could be the child's room, the dining room table, or any quiet part of the house. Be consistent with this so that once the child finds herself in that particular place, she knows automatically that it's time for serious business. Consistency is said to be a key to success.
- Ensure that supplies (pencils, erasers, pens, etc.) are available and handy for the child all the time. A home dictionary is essential—provide one and encourage your child to use it, although, these days, children find it more convenient to consult online dictionaries.
- Set an amount of time for study or homework. In doing this, consider your child's developmental level. While secondary school students can focus for over an hour, elementary pupils are not likely to sit for that long on a single task. You may want to allow for short breaks in between, perhaps as a reward for finishing a section of the work.
- Find ways to motivate your child to do his best. Children respond well when you give them something to look forward to. It could be playtime with a friend after the work is done or anything you can come up with that the child likes to do. More importantly, teach your child that studying involves more than just doing homework. The difference between studying and doing homework is often misunderstood. Studying is a habit we should help

our children cultivate. Whether or not they have homework, they should make time to study their schoolwork and also do lots of general reading.

During a homework session, watch out for signs of frustration. No learning can take place and only very little can be accomplished if the child is angry or upset over an assignment that takes too long to finish or is too difficult. At such times, you may have to step in. Find out where the frustration is coming from, and see if it is something you can help with. Otherwise, to avoid getting the child more confused, simply stop the homework for that day and write a note to the teacher explaining the situation and requesting that he or she goes over the work once more with your child to help her understand it better.

I remember one particular time when our older daughter brought out her homework to do. I first noticed that she was unusually sluggish about it, and then I saw that she was making several mistakes she would not usually make, so I had to step in. I tried to find out what the problem was and she simply told me that she was tired. First I thought about the fact that being up-to-date in their assignments kept them in the teacher's good books, and I was always afraid of them being vulnerable. Again, I thought about what was best for my child at that time. She was tired and just could not get anything productive done, and I knew that a little rest would help. I decided that she should discontinue the work. The next morning I sent a note to the teacher and pleaded with her to allow her turn in the work the following day. She had double work to do the following evening, but she was able to do the work with ease because she was relaxed.

I had a situation with my son also, where he had come home with French homework. I could tell immediately that there was a problem as I watched him open his workbook and begin to write with a confused look on his face. I stopped him halfway through and looked at his book—some of the words he had written in his book to match the pictures were similar to words we had come across in Spanish. I thought he might be confusing French with Spanish. He had learned Spanish in his previous school, but when he got to this new school, he had to switch to French because it was the only foreign language taught in the school. Looking at the workbook in front of him, he got confused and began to mix French words with Spanish. I thought to myself that he couldn't continue with that confusion, but I could not help him since I couldn't speak any of the languages, so I stopped the session.

I wrote a note to the French teacher the following day, explaining the situation to him and why my little boy did not do the assignment. I requested that he please take my son through the basics, since he was not there at the beginning of the school year and had missed many lessons. I also requested he recommend books we could buy and use to work with our son at home. I let the teacher know that I was ready to work with him to achieve a positive result and then thanked him for his cooperation. The teacher, after reading my note, was very impressed and glad there was a mother who cared, not just about math or science, but about French—which according to him, many people did not take very seriously. Knowing he had my cooperation, he committed to ensuring that my son overcame the challenge.

In summarizing this chapter, the need for parents to work with their children's teachers/schools cannot be overemphasized. Keep an open mind, and be optimistic. Seek ways to help the teacher help your child, and provide useful information about your child to the teacher. When issues arise, work with the teacher to resolve them. Let your child also know that you and the teacher are a team in ensuring her academic success.

5

FITNESS AND DIET FOR CHILDREN

*If we could give every individual the right amount of nourish-
ment and exercise, not too little and not too much, we would
have found the safest way to health.*

—HIPPOCRATES

STILL DRAWING ON our example from the life of Jesus in Luke 2:52, the physical growth of our children is very important to their overall growth and well-being. Proper physical growth helps to foster positive self-esteem. A child with stunted growth or who suffers from malnutrition is prone to ridicule from his peers. On the other hand, a child who is suffering from obesity will also face ridicule and poor health.

According to the Centers for Disease Control and Prevention, childhood obesity has more than doubled in children and tripled in adolescents in the past thirty years.[5] The percentage of children aged six

---

5 "Childhood Obesity Facts," CDC. Last modified August 27, 2015. http://www.cdc.gov/healthyyouth/obesity/facts.htm

to eleven years in the United States who were obese increased from 7 percent in 1980 to nearly 18 percent in 2010. Similarly, the percentage of adolescents aged twelve to nineteen years that were obese increased from 5 percent to 18 percent over the same period. This is scary!

Children need balanced nutrition to nurture their physical health and growth. This not only prevents nutrient deficiency in children but also promotes a healthy and active life. Balanced nutrition, good eating habits, and appropriate exercise during infancy and childhood are important for the growth and development of the child.

Growth is defined as an increase in size. *Development* is defined as a progression toward maturity. Thus, the terms (growth and development) are used together to describe the complex physical, mental, and emotional processes associated with the "growing up" of children.[6] Growth is continuous from birth to maturity and is therefore considered an important indicator of a child's nutritional status. In other words, nutrition is an extremely important environmental factor that affects the growth and development of a child. Well-nourished children are often able to reach the potential set by their heredity, both in terms of physical and mental health. Children need healthy meals and exercise to grow properly.

BALANCED NUTRITION

"The nutrition a child receives during the first few years of life can affect her health for years to come. Balanced nutrition is important to child development because children need specific nutrients to thrive and grow. Poor nutrition can result from lack of food as well as overeating, since nutrition is about more than simple caloric intake. Proper child development relies on a solid nutritional foundation, which includes the correct amount of each nutrient."[7] It is extremely important to ensure

6 "Growth," Medical-Dictionary.com. Last modified on December 3, 2013. http://www.medical-dictionary.thefreedictionary.com/growth

7 "How Poor Nutrition Affects Child Development," Dakota Karratti. Last modified on April 24, 2015. http://www.livestrong.com/article/465374-how-poor-nutrition-affects-child-development/

that whatever you put on the table for your child supports her proper growth and development.

The term "balanced diet" is a common term that describes a meal that includes all essential nutrients: carbohydrates, protein, vitamins, minerals, fats, and oil. A balanced diet combines these various nutrients in the right proportion. Foods are grouped into various categories to make it a little easier: fruit and vegetables, grains and cereals, dairy products and calcium sources, meat and protein sources, and fats and oils. Each of these groups contains a large number of varieties. Consider these nutrient-dense foods:

- **Protein:** These can be found in seafood, lean meat and poultry, eggs, beans, peas, soy products, and unsalted nuts and seeds.
- **Fruits:** Encourage your child to eat a variety of fresh, canned, frozen, and dried fruits, rather than fruit juice. If your child drinks juice, make sure it's 100 percent juice and limit his servings.
- **Vegetables:** Serve a variety of fresh, canned, or frozen vegetables, especially dark green, red, and orange vegetables, beans, and peas.
- **Grains:** Choose whole grains, such as whole wheat bread, oatmeal, popcorn, quinoa, or brown or wild rice.
- **Dairy:** Encourage your child to eat and drink fat-free or low-fat dairy products, such as milk, yogurt, cheese, or fortified soy beverages.

Aim to limit the number of calories your child gets from solid fats and sugars, such as butter, cake, and carbonated drinks. Look for ways to replace solid fats with vegetable and nut oils, which provide essential fatty acids and vitamin E. Oils are naturally present in olives, nuts, avocados, and seafood.[8] Water is also very essential to the body. It helps

---

8 "Nutrition for Kids: Guidelines for a Healthy Diet," Mayo Clinic. Last modified January 16, 2016. http://www.mayoclinic.org/healthy-lifestyle/childrens-health/in-depth/nutrition-for-kids/art-20049335

maintain a constant internal body temperature and transports nutrients to cells. It also assists in removing waste products from the body. Encourage your child to drink more water and reduce the consumption of carbonated drinks and unnatural juices.

Healthy meals are not necessarily expensive. A good knowledge of what nutrients your child's body needs for proper growth is vital in trying to provide healthy meals for your family. Let me emphasize that fruits and vegetables are essential for a good supply of minerals and vitamins. Even though they are not your children's favorites, they should always be part of their meals.

Children do not need to be placed on any special diet (except where there is a need for it, where it is directed by a dietician), but they need to cultivate a healthy eating lifestyle. They need to eat the right kind of foods and should be trained to know what they should eat, when to eat, and the right proportions they should consume for proper growth. This calls for discipline. It is especially important that you as the parent set a good example for your children with your food choices and your attitude toward food. As they grow up, you'll have less control over what they eat, so help them develop good eating habits early on and hope they stay with it. Provide wholesome food for your children and help them form the habit of healthy eating. Children by nature will prefer "junk food," and peer pressure and the TV commercials for junk food make it even worse. When you introduce a healthy meal, your children might not like it initially, but if you find ways to motivate them, they will eventually come to like these meals. Children develop a natural preference for the foods they enjoy the most, so the challenge is to make healthy choices appealing.

Growing up during the austerity era in Nigeria, I saw my mum get really creative with food just to make sure we had the right quality of food, with all the essential nutrients our body needed to grow. Mum is that kind of woman described in Proverbs 31; she knew what to put together with limited resources to give us very balanced and healthy meals. I remember that during the same era food was very expensive;

rice, for example, became the food of the rich. During that time, corn was available and was very affordable, so my mum maximized the use of corn. She made wonderful meals out of corn; she could make a 1,001 delicacies with corn and always fortified it with lots of fresh vegetables, prawns, and fish (for the needed nutrients). She made milk from soya beans and provided plenty of fruits, which kept us very healthy.

Mothers, you have to be creative with what you put on the table for your family. Prepare meals with purpose in mind. Be sure that each time you present food to your child you have included all the basic nutrients your child needs for healthy growth. Ensure your child's diet supports a healthy life.

BREAKFAST: START YOUR CHILD'S DAY OFF RIGHT

Multiple studies show that children who eat breakfast every day have better memories, experience more stable moods and energy, score higher on tests, and miss fewer days from school. They are also less likely to experience problems with their weight.[9]

Breakfast is said to be the most important meal of the day; it is therefore important to ensure your child eats breakfast before setting out for school in the morning. This helps them start off their day with plenty of energy. Do not send your child off to school in the morning without a good breakfast. A child in the classroom whose last meal was dinner the night before has gone about fifteen to eighteen hours without food, and that child is hungry, whether he thinks so or not. A nutritious breakfast will provide energy for several hours until lunchtime.

Is any kind of breakfast better than no breakfast at all? Unfortunately, no! A doughnut or sugarcoated cereal, for example, provides a quick rush of energy that only lasts about forty minutes, which is about the length of time it takes the child to get to school. Children need "brain

---

9 "Nutrition for Children and Teens," Maya W. Paul and Lawrence Robertson. Last modified February 2016. http://helpguide.org/articles/healthy-eating/nutrition-for-children-and-teens.htm

food," especially in the morning. Eating a breakfast high in quality protein can help overweight teenagers eat fewer calories throughout the rest of the day and lose weight. The ideal breakfast features plenty of good carbohydrates (fruit, whole grain toast, or cereal, for example), as well as high-quality protein.[10] High-quality proteins are brain foods; they improve memory, mood, concentration, and overall clarity. They keep the mind sharp and nourished. Protein-rich foods include fish, lean meat, eggs, milk, nuts, and whole grain.

Traditionally, teachers schedule brain-tasking subjects, like math and English, in the morning hours, and so it becomes even more important that the child's brain is nourished. While cereals are fast and easy to prepare in the morning, make sure they are whole grain and avoid cereals that are coated with excessive sugar (although those are the ones the children prefer). When you serve your children cereal in the morning, give it an extra boost with a sprinkling of nuts and fruit, fresh or dry.

[I encourage you to do more research to understand what kinds of food will be right for your child and then begin to provide meals that will only foster good health. If your child has special dietary needs, you might want to see a dietician.]

SNACK TIME

The need to help our children develop a healthy eating lifestyle cannot be overemphasized. Children ordinarily like to snack rather than eat proper food. There is a place for snacks and a place for proper meals. It is OK to provide snacks for your children in between their meals, as they burn off a lot of energy during play and often need to refuel. However, the type of snacks you make available to them is crucial. Rather than unhealthy salty crisps, sugar-filled sour punch, and the like, you can provide snacks that are much healthier and that your children will still like.

The way I've been able to promote healthy snacking in our home is by making only healthy snacks available. Seasonal fruits make healthy

---

10   Ibid.

snacks as well, for instance. And when fruits are in season, they are fresh, available, and affordable. Mangoes, tangerines, apples, carrots and grapes are some of the fruits children like and can snack on. One of our favorites is groundnut (peanut), preferably boiled, in its shell. Our children still love to crack the shells, which makes it extra fun to eat. They particularly enjoyed it while watching TV, and we substitute it for popcorn sometimes.

HYPERACTIVITY AND DIET

Some children are restless, excessively playful, and very easily distracted,—some of the symptoms of hyperactivity in children. Unfortunately, children who are really hyperactive often find it difficult to control their actions and are always in trouble for unintended behaviors. As a purposeful parent, you should be well informed about your child's situation and know when there is a problem in order to provide the appropriate support your child needs. Hyperactivity is often associated with learning disorders. Logically, when a child is too playful and easily distracted, he loses focus and concentration, which begins to affect him academically. So if hyperactivity is not controlled in children, it can eventually be very destructive. I have found proper diet to be helpful in reducing hyperactivity in children.

I realized long ago that what a child eats has the potential to aggravate her level of activity. Children who seem to be hyperactive and very restless do not need excessive sugar in their system; instead they need more brain food to help them focus. They also need structured exercise to help them burn off excess energy. Sugar is an enemy of your child and often aggravates hyperactivity. If you take the time to observe, you will realize that your child's behavior deteriorates after eating high-sugar foods such as cakes, sugar cookies, and the like, and when they consume carbonated and caffeinated soft drinks. I am not suggesting that children should be deprived of these completely. However, the frequency and timing of consumption are important factors to consider in managing your child's hyperactivity. We have had to completely take out sugar and caffeinated and carbonated drinks at a certain point, and this did work for us.

PHYSICAL FITNESS

Children need to combine good nutrition and physical exercise for healthy physical growth. When we burn energy, we also gain energy. Therefore, it is necessary to provide sufficient opportunity for your child to engage in physical play in order to maintain good physical development and health. Fortunately, exercise for children does not require much, as children can easily create active fun for themselves. Simply creating the opportunity and environment for children to engage in physical activities and release their excess energy will do the trick. This could involve riding bicycles around the neighborhood, playing tag with other children, jumping rope, playing ball, or engaging in sports at school.

I am of the opinion that children should spend more time in physical play than they spend watching television or playing video games. I found it very helpful to let my children go outside and play, because I realized they were full of energy, and when they were not able to release that excess energy, they began to "act up." I also realized that taking time to play with my children was good for my health as well. I burned a lot of calories running around and playing with my children. You try playing catch or racing in the pool with a ten-year-old, and you will understand what I am talking about.

At this point, I must encourage parents to be open to new things and to stay involved in your children's lives. Don't feel so sophisticated that you are unable to come down to their level and enjoy some "playtime" with your children. They need you to be available and to connect with them emotionally. Create opportunity for interaction with your children, and learn to laugh together. That is where you connect with them, and by doing that, you will be meeting their emotional needs as well as your own. It is important to enjoy every stage of your child's life.

When our children were younger, we made a serious effort to be involved in their activities as much as possible, which made me feel like they were helping me live my childhood over again. I found it to be very true that "while we try to teach our children about life, they teach us what life is all about." They taught me love, patience, and what fun is all about. They gave me the opportunity to learn to do things I never did growing up. This might sound ridiculous, but my children taught me how to ride a bicycle. I never had the opportunity to swim until our first child was four years old. I was motivated to learn to swim when one of our children almost drowned in a pool; then I realized that swimming was a life skill everyone should have.

It was the scariest experience of my life. Our Bible study small group leader had invited the group of five families to her home for a get-together. It was a pool party. I couldn't swim at the time, but since they had a baby pool attached to their main pool and there would be quite a number of adults who were good swimmers right in the pool, we decided to allow our son to play with the other little children in the baby pool. While the kids played, the adults and older children were in the main pool playing volleyball while the rest of us were chatting on the patio. I could not keep my eyes off our son as I watched him stare at the adults playing ball in the main pool. He loved balls and still does. He stared so much that he became eager to join in the play, and within a split second, I watched him jump into the five-to-nine-foot-deep pool, reaching for the ball. Immediately, I began to scream for help. Unfortunately, the people in the pool were engrossed in their play and had no idea what had happened. Also, the noise from the flowing fountain in the pool made it even more difficult for anyone to hear me. At that moment, our hostess stepped out of the house through the kitchen door and immediately dove in and picked him up. To God be the glory!

I was so grateful to God. I thought to myself that if there had been no one to rescue him, I would have helplessly watched my son drown in the pool. God forbid! I had two options: nurse the phobia I was beginning to develop for water based on that experience and as a result stop my children from ever going near a swimming pool, or overcome that fear and allow my children to continue to learn to swim. We purposefully chose to allow them continue to develop their swimming skills, as we then began to see swimming as a necessary life skill. However, since they were still very young, I knew I'd be more comfortable if I could be in the pool with them while they swam, as I realized that even lifeguards are sometimes distracted. This led me to a decision: I also needed to learn how to swim so I decided to take swimming lessons until I was comfortable and could swim the whole length of a standard swimming pool, up to twelve feet. Then as young as six months old, I began to take my youngest child into the swimming pool, and by the age of three (and with a couple of structured lessons), she was already a good swimmer. Today, we all swim comfortably in pools as deep as twelve feet, and we all enjoy swimming together without fear. Swimming has become my favorite workout; it keeps me in shape, thanks to my wonderful three.

When you get involved with your children and provide opportunities for healthy play, you will not only be raising healthy children but building a close-knit family while getting a workout yourself.

6

TACKLING SOCIAL VICES

Safety and security don't just happen; they are the result of collective consensus and public investment. We owe our children, the most vulnerable citizens in our society, a life free of violence and fear.

—NELSON MANDELA

CHILDREN ARE MEANT to be guided and directed, but in order to help your children develop and live a balanced social life, you must assume the role of a manager. A manager in the home is simply one who directs household affairs. In managing our children, we are not merely talking about getting them civilized. Managing your child is not like managing a business. As a manager of your child, you need to consider the emotional, relational, and spiritual issues that affect him.

Children's personalities, emotions, and social skills differ, and are influenced by the guidance they receive. Children learn social behaviors by imitating their parents, other children, and other people around them; hence, social and emotional skills should be taught/learned. Young children especially need the help of their parents to adjust their emotions to the current situation. Therefore, it is helpful for parents to provide appropriate and healthy social interactions for children, and this means creating opportunities for her to meet and play with other children. In providing these opportunities, it is vital that you as the parent define and agree on limits with your child. Children need a lot of guidance, because they are children and by their nature should be guided. That is why the Bible says: *"Foolishness is bound up in the heart of a child…"* (Proverbs 22:15a).

When your child invites friends over to your home for a playdate, it is important that you make yourself available or ensure appropriate adult supervision for the children. Your presence or the presence of a designated responsible adult in the home provides some level of safety for all the children. While you do not have to get in their faces, you must be visible enough to restrain the children from mischief. As a counselor, I have had the opportunity to listen to children explain how they picked up certain bad habits (sometimes good habits, too). Habits can be picked up from anywhere, but we owe it to our children and their friends to ensure their safety while in our home.

PARTY AND VISITING ETHICS

These days, children arrange visits without involving their parents in the plan. Say your child comes home and tells you that she and her friends have a playdate planned at one of her friend's houses. The first thing to ask is whether the friend's mum is aware that the children are coming over to play and if she is ready for it. It is vital that, before you send your child to someone's house, the parents are aware your child is coming and have approved of it. Ideally, the host mum should call to invite your child over. For example, if my child wants to have her friends over, she should let me know. It's not enough for me to say that it's OK, but I should be courteous enough to call the parents of the other children to invite them over. On the other hand, if your child chooses to go visit a friend, it is only proper that you call the friend's parents to ensure that it is OK for your child to visit at the time and not just send your child over because her friend says it's OK. The parents might have other plans, and we should be considerate. If the visit cannot happen at that time, it could happen some other time. Young children should not be left unsupervised, even at home.

Another thing we take for granted as parents sometimes is party invitations. When your child has been invited to a party, do not take siblings along without checking with the host parents to make sure it is OK. When parents plan parties for their children, they usually prepare for a certain number of children and organize activities for a particular age range. If they have more children than they have prepared for, it could throw them into a panic (such as when they realize they don't have enough gift bags) and disrupt party plans. Sometimes you can't avoid having your other child tagging along for a party her sibling has been invited to, especially when logistics come into play. But call ahead of time and let the host parent know so that she can make adequate preparations. Likewise, when your child has been invited to a party and is not able to attend, courtesy demands that you call and let the other parents know that your child will not be coming. It is only proper. Also, try not to send your child to a party without a present or at least a card, even if it is a handmade card by your child. It shows that your child had put some thought into the invitation.

Let us teach our children and model to them the proper way to socialize. They should learn not to attend parties or go to places they have not been invited. They should, at a very young age, be taught these values.

SLEEPOVERS
Children often plan playdates with their friends and simply get their parents to stamp it with an approval, sometimes without even knowing

who these friends are. One such social gathering that children enjoy is the sleepover. Sleepovers are very popular among children, and every child wants to go to one or host one. Personally, I am not a fan of sleepovers. I believe children should play in the daytime and sleep at night. However, if your child is attending a sleepover, here are some points to consider:

- Consider the spiritual atmosphere of the home your child will be staying at overnight. You don't want to expose her to any spiritual contamination because you don't know what happens, even in decent-looking modern homes. Growing up, I had a friend I played with in the neighborhood, and we visited each other's homes. We never slept over, but the visits were frequent. I was about eleven at the time, and I noticed that whenever I was in their house and my friend's mum wanted to cook chicken, a dead chicken would appear from her bedroom. She would always come out of her bedroom with an already killed chicken to cook, and I thought there was something wrong with that picture. Then I got curious. One day as we were playing around, I followed my friend into her mum's bedroom and noticed a red curtain drawn across a corner of the room, and so I asked my friend what was behind the curtain. She casually told me that it was their family shrine. They had dealings with "some evil spirit," so they made sacrifices to it in that shrine, and at night her mum would often go to their room while they were sleeping to invoke the spirit in the house and over them. (How many times do you as a Christian parent go around while your children are sleeping to lay your hand over them and speak the purpose of God into their lives?) That then explained where the dead chicken was coming from, as they often made sacrifices on that shrine to their god. Now when I think about sleepovers, I wonder whether if I had slept over in that house, they would have been invoking that spirit over me, too!

- Inquire about the level of adult supervision during a sleepover. How many parents will willingly lose sleep and stay up overnight to supervise the children they have invited into their home? There needs to be a certain level of supervision that not all parents take the time to provide. Children are often left to themselves to explore all kinds of things through the night. I often imagine what kind of movies show overnight (which children might be tempted to stay up for most of the night watching), when during the day it is hard to find a good program to watch on the television.
- Get to know the parents before a potential sleepover. Have a chat with the mum, or invite the child over for a daytime playdate. Let's learn to take baby steps to understand who we are dealing with instead of suddenly letting our children loose with a couple of other children at somebody's house. It is also reasonable to ask or inquire about the other children who will be attending.
- If your child is hosting a sleepover, make yourself available to supervise the children and ensure their safety in your home. This does not mean getting in their face, but the thought of you being around and popping in from time to time will keep the children in check. Define clear boundaries: make them realistic and reasonable, and also enforce them. It will be the duty of your child to let her friends know the rules before they come over.

My daughter attended her first and probably only sleepover party when she was eight years old, even though she had been invited to several previously. I couldn't imagine not having her at home in her bed that night. However, I felt a release to allow her go—more so with the confidence that the host mum (someone I knew very well) would take good care of the children. It was her friend's birthday, and the mum had planned a weekend of fun and learning for the five little girls she had invited. She did not let the girls out of her sight, and when they were ready to sleep, she had all the girls sleep in her room, and she watched over them like a mother hen, forfeiting her own sleep. That is the kind of sacrifice mothers will have to make when they host sleepovers, especially when the children are young and impressionable.

Some parents have argued that the only reason parents won't allow their child to have a sleepover is due to a lack of trust in that child. Well, they may be right in some cases, but I also know from my interaction with adolescents who have been victims of molestation that sometimes children find themselves in helpless situations, and certain things have happened to "good, well-brought-up, and trusted" children without their consent. This is not to say that bad things happen at every sleepover; rather, it is your responsibility as the parent to discern the environment.

TEACH YOUR CHILD TO MAKE THE RIGHT CHOICES

While we do what we can to protect our children from negative exposures and influences, it's most important that we build in them the confidence to make the right choices when they find themselves in compromising situations. I think this is very important in purposeful parenting. Children experience social challenges among their peers and are faced with negative peer pressure. In helping your child develop and maintain a stable social life, you should consider working on her self-esteem early on, as addressed in chapter 2.

What should be our focus? Each time I ask myself this question, I remember a radio drama I listened to on the Christian radio station KSBJ some years back, where a nine-year-old girl went to a sleepover party at a friend's house, and around midnight the girls decided to watch a movie that was inappropriate for their age. She knew that her parents would not approve of it and voted against it, but most of the girls wanted to see the movie so they got the approval of the host mum (clash of values). This girl was uncomfortable in that environment, so she called her dad to come pick her up immediately. Her dad came over and brought her back home.

There is a valuable lesson here. Can we raise our children to the level where even in our absence they are able to maintain the values we teach and that they believe in? How do we raise children who understand who they are and are confident of it, irrespective of what the greater percentage of their friends think? This nine-year-old girl could have seen this as an opportunity to indulge herself since her parents were not there—just like many children who do not want to be the odd ones out. You can tell this little girl had very strong positive self-esteem and cared little about what her friends thought or how they would feel about her values. She was more concerned about what mattered to her and the standards her family upheld. This is the level we should desire for our children: that they would be able to say no when they should. We need to teach our children that it is OK to say no and not to be intimidated when their views and values are not popular.

The irony, though, is that many of us (parents) fall for peer pressure ourselves, and our children mirror us. We allow things because "everyone is doing it." We want our children to be seen to be flowing along. As a parent, it's critical that you develop good personal values and create a standard that is consistent with your values. Let your children understand why you do things the way you do. You are not in competition with anybody; you have a purpose you want to achieve.

HELPING CHILDREN KEEP SAFE

The safety of your child must be a priority as you make your way along the parenting journey. Children contend with all kinds of negative influences and should be protected from such influences. The world is becoming more perverse. Things are done out of order, and a lot of children are made to believe that these things are the norm.

The Bible says, *"But while men slept, his enemy came and sowed tares among the wheat, and went his way"* (Matthew 13:25). It appears that many parents today are sleeping and allowing the enemy to sow evil seeds in the lives of their children. As you read this book, consider it a wake-up call. The alarm is ringing. It is time to wake up, to be real and watchful, and to protect your children from this enemy whose only mission is to steal, kill, and destroy. While "parents sleep," children are being introduced to drugs, sex, pornography, masturbation, lesbianism, homosexuality, witchcraft, and the like. "Sleep" in this context means that parents are too busy and distracted with so many other things that they do not see the dangers their children are faced with.

Bad things don't only happen outside the home; it shouldn't surprise you that right under the watchful eyes of parents, incest is taking place in homes. Children are being molested and abused by the trusted adults parents have asked to watch them: nannies, drivers, uncles, aunties, neighbors, and so on. You hear over and over again how drivers fiddle with the bodies of little girls right inside the car, yet some parents still leave their children alone with drivers. We hear stories about how even babies are being molested. These appalling stories go on and on, and they are very real. It is sad that many parents still don't believe that these things happen.

You must make your home a safe haven for your children. When they go out into their world each day, they are exposed to a lot of things out there. They should be able to see a difference between the kinds of exposure they have at home and what they experience outside the home. One thing I often tell my children when they come complaining about things they heard or saw people do in school, at birthday parties, and so on is that the world will not shut down for them. I let them understand it as the way today's world is, and then I tell them that even though they are in this world, they are not of the world. They can be different! This world is full of negative influences and sadly will not get any better, but they have to commit to being different. When children have gone through a day of so much hassle, they should be able to come back home to an environment that is safe, secure, pure, and full of love.

Your children should always look forward to coming home where they feel safe, secure, and loved under your care. But when the home is not secure—when after going through all the ordeals outside, they come back home to an environment that is equally unsafe, with one uncle who should be helping at home molesting them instead—then there is nowhere for the child to run. And "when they can't beat them, they are forced to join them."

SEXUALITY EDUCATION

It is sad that with the alarming rate of child sexual abuse, parents still deny that these things happen and are not even ready to talk about them with their children. Bear in mind that if you don't talk about drugs, alcohol, sex, and such to your children, they will still hear about these things anyway but from the wrong sources, and they will often be fed the wrong information. I believe that the earlier we talk to our children about these things, the better equipped they will be to handle such issues if they arise. Begin to talk to your children about sex, drugs, alcohol, and other vices. Sexuality education is one of the most effective preventive measures to take in protecting our children against sexual abuse.

Children should be taught that they have the right not to allow anyone to defile their bodies—that their bodies are the temple of the Holy Spirit and should be kept pure. As parents, we should develop a relationship with our children where they are able to talk to us about anything. Children often do not report these issues because of fear of what their parents might do or say, so they keep quiet, giving their predators the opportunity to continue to molest them. Predators will often threaten to harm their victims and/or their family if they tell anybody. Talk about these issues freely with your children, and continue to assure them of your love. Let them know they can trust you and talk to you about anything. And when they do, you must handle your children's issues with care.

Likewise, you cannot afford to be naïve as a parent. Wake up from your slumber, and watch out for sexual activities within your household. Children are not usually molested by strangers but by people within the household. Teach your children to maintain their personal space, avoid questionable privacies, and communicate abusive tendencies. You should also be sensitive and watch out for signs of abuse, including:

- The child exhibits fear of certain people and places. This is not the time to insist that your child hug an uncle or visit an aunty he is not comfortable with, irrespective of who or where. When a child begins to withdraw from family, friends, or usual activities, this could be a sign.
- The child exhibits advanced sexual knowledge (when you haven't taught it). In this case, you might want to ask some questions to understand where such knowledge is coming from.

Understand that sexual abuse can be a cycle that keeps recurring if not stopped. It leads to "learned helplessness," where children feel like they are helpless and after a while begin to enjoy the act or exposure. (Sexual abuse may not involve body contact; exposure to inappropriate sexual materials is also an abuse.) Abuse can make people feel like they are helpless. If you suspect that your child has been or is being abused, you must step in and break the cycle. If you don't, your child may develop low self-esteem, loss of confidence, unstable emotions, homosexual tendencies, or depression, and/or contract sexually transmitted diseases (STDs).

Parents are often unable to deal with these issues by themselves, but this is not a reason to live in denial or sweep it under the carpet. If it is not dealt with appropriately and swiftly, the child will grow into dependency. It is important that as a parent you are aware of the child protection laws where you live and ensure you have the relevant contact information to report cases of child abuse. Many abuse cases are never reported because of social stigma. It is important to report these cases and allow the law to deal with them. By doing so, you will be preventing that predator from continuing to hurt your child and other children. Find out how your state deals with such cases and where to make the report.

Remember, the self-esteem of your child is the most important factor, so see a counselor and/or seek appropriate help for your child. Better yet, parents need to be proactive in matters of abuse, as prevention is said to be better than the cure. Begin educating your children in sexuality early on. Teach them about their bodies, and let them know that God created them beautifully and made certain parts of their bodies private, meaning that no other person is meant to see or touch those parts (their chests, genitals, buttocks, laps, and so on). Mention the parts to them, including their lips. Teach them to keep their bodies safe and to never allow anyone to touch any part of their bodies that should be private.

Generally, children should only be given as much information as they can handle. The way you teach sexuality education to a three-year-old is not the same way you would a ten-year-old, but all children should be taught. Start early and tell them the bit they need to know and can handle, and then open it up more as they get older. Most importantly, teach your children to tell you whenever anyone tries to make them feel uncomfortable. There have been stories where the "neighbor next door" molested children who came over to play with their own children. Did you say sick? Yes, sick! Teach your children who strangers are. In our family, we define strangers as people who are not members of our immediate family, and it stays that way, especially in societies where everyone is "brother and sister" or "uncle and aunty." We must equip our children with all the information they need for their safety and protection, and to survive in life. There is a lot we have to talk to our children about. We must find a way to educate and equip them with necessary information in a way they can understand. Children are very impressionable and vulnerable.

As Christian parents, do not relent in preaching the message of abstinence to your children, especially your adolescents. The Bible says, *Flee sexual immorality. Every sin that a man does is outside the body, but he who commits sexual immorality sins against his own body. Or do you not know that your body is the temple of the Holy Spirit who is in you, whom you have from God, and you are not your own? For you were bought at a price; therefore glorify*

God in your body and in your spirit, which are God's. (1 Corinthians 6:18-20). No matter what society says today, children and adolescents should be taught the truth of the word of God. Otherwise, they will believe the lies of the devil by accepting what seems to be the norm of the society. Children should be taught early before they ignorantly begin to expose themselves to things contrary to the word of God.

SMOKING, DRUGS, AND ALCOHOL

These are usually habits and addictions that often start with one curious experiment. Talk to your children about these habits and their dangers. It is never too early to teach them about dangers of these things.

When our older children were about four and six years old, my husband took time to talk to them about smoking. At that time I thought it was too early, but he explained to me that we didn't have control of what society released to them. Rather, we only had control of the values we instilled in them. I can't remember exactly how it started, but I remember we were in the car going somewhere when one of the children asked a question when he saw someone smoking on the street, so my husband used that opportunity to talk to them extensively about it. His goal was to deal with it objectively so that they would understand the dangers of smoking, especially to human health, and detest it, even from childhood. First, he established that it was unhealthy (it makes people sick), and because it is unhealthy, people who smoke are harming their lungs. He explained that God is not happy about this, because our bodies are God's temple and God is not happy with anyone who tampers with His temple (1 Corinthians 3:16–17).

Later on when an opportunity came up to talk about it again, he used a practical example to explain it further to them. He lit a smoky charcoal grill and put a very clean kettle of water on it. After a while, they noticed that the kettle got darker with the smoke. So he explained to them that when a person smokes, after some time (it might be a short period or a long period of time), the lungs begin to get darker than they should be and the person may get sick and die. Some years later I came across the picture of the lungs of a smoker on the Internet, I printed it out and also printed a picture of healthy lungs, and they compared the two. They got the picture. The idea is, teach your children what you want them to learn before society teaches them the wrong things. If it is important, then teach it.

In tackling social vices, it is important to also employ parental control—not just on the computer and Internet, but also on the books children read, songs they listen to, and movies they watch. The eyes and ears are gates to our body. When children read books or watch movies that are too graphic for their age, they are exposed to fear and tend to have nightmares or disturbed sleep. For reviews of movies, books, TV shows, and more, pluggedin.com is a good reference and resource.

BACK TO THE KEEPER

Beyond the importance of parental care and engaging our parental instincts, we must at all times commit the safety and protection of our children to God's hands. This is the ultimate gesture! I have learned that "if God cannot keep my children, then I cannot keep them either."

MENTORING YOUR CHILD

Children need mentors as much as adults do, people they can look up to for direction and whose lifestyle will challenge and influence them positively. You are the greatest mentor your child can ever have because you have a genuine interest and a stake in the progress of your child. In performing the role of a mentor to your child, you assume the part of a role model. Realize that you are your child's hero. When you ask children, they will often say that they want to be like their mummy or daddy. Children are born without any social knowledge or skills, and they eagerly look for someone to imitate, which is usually the parent. By virtue of your God-given position as the parent, you are your child's first teacher and role model. Children are more affected by what they see their parents do than anything else. They learn how to behave by watching how their parents behave, and they follow their examples, whether good or bad.

From infancy, your children watch you. They learn from your actions and your conversations. They absorb your attitudes and copy your expressions. And before they are of school age, they have probably learned more than you ever intended. What they watch you do goes a long way in affecting how they view life and sometimes who they become. Children like to copy, and they will copy everything you do, whether good or bad. Have you ever said a curse word in front of your child, only to hear her repeating that word later on (usually at the worst possible time)? Children are very impressionable and highly imitative with both words and actions. You need to be a strong, consistent, and positive influence on your child.

Some parents still practice the theory of "do as I say and not as I do," but it does not work that way. You have to live what you preach, "walk your talk," because believe it or not, you will make a huge impression on your children, be it positive or negative. There is no better way to model positive behavior to your children and boost their self-confidence than by using social skills. A child learns good manners easily when "please" and "thank you" are a part of his daily family life. When you have the habit of putting other people down, you are simply teaching your children that others are not important. If you want your child to respect people, you must yourself, respect your child, and respect others as well. Encourage all family members to treat one another with respect. Even the domestic workers in your household deserve respect. The best way your children can learn respect is to see you respect people.

Likewise, teach good morals to your children by shaping up your own moral life. Don't ignore bad behavior thinking it does not matter; it might not seem to matter at that point in time, but the consequences will definitely show up some day. Setting good examples is very important. Sometimes we lose our tempers and say things we are not supposed to say, and are not always as kind as we should be. Always admit your mistakes, apologize, and make efforts to correct the situation. Being a positive role model for your children is one of the most rewarding things you can ever do for them.

Let me say here that there is no such thing as the "perfect parent," because I consider parenting the world's most challenging job. While we appreciate the special joy of raising children, we also know that it can be the most demanding and exhausting thing you'll ever do. Some days you are at your best as a parent, doing a great job, and other days you would rather not think about it. But the irony is that *every day* you act as a model to your children in any situation you find yourself in. Other people can also serve as role models to your child, including grandparents, aunts, uncles, teachers, and neighbors. Just one positive caring adult can make a difference in your child's life, and the more positive examples your child has to learn from, the better. Exhibit godly characters for your children to emulate. It is not enough to set boundaries for your children when you are without boundaries yourself. They are watching you and want to do what you do.

For instance, when you employ the services of domestic workers in your home, this is a good and practical opportunity for your children to learn how to humble themselves and show appreciation and respect for people. It is important for children to understand that their nanny, the family's driver, the steward, and the cook are just as important to God as they are and should be treated with respect. Again, the way you as the parent relate with these domestic staff members will also determine how your children will relate to them.

We had a young man who came in once in a week to do our cleaning and laundry. He always did an excellent job for us and often took initiatives, and was very honest and trustworthy. He turned out to be a great help to us. Although he was being paid for the work he did, I often thought to myself that if he were not available to do the work, the money we paid him would not grow hands to do the work for us. So I learned to respect him for who he was and the wonderful work he did for us. I appreciated him and thanked him as if he did the work for no charge. Soon our children learned to appreciate him as well. They would come back from school to see their rooms neat and tidy, sparkling clean, and their clothes washed and well ironed, and they would run to him (if he was still around) to say, "Thank you for cleaning our rooms." This even motivated the young man to do more. He would even go out of his way to wash our cars without being asked and for no additional charge. When we appreciate people, it helps to bring out the best in them.

In summarizing this chapter, it is important to keep the communication line open between you and your children at all times. When there is open communication before anything goes wrong, your child is more likely to discuss her feelings with you. Educate your children properly at home; when you do, they are not likely to be deceived outside. We have a duty to our children to help them arm themselves with the knowledge, information, and skills required to survive the pressures that life, society, and peers bring.

7

Spiritual Foundation

Every child you encounter is a divine appointment.

—Wess Stafford

ALL ASPECTS OF a human's life—his or her character, sense of responsibility, habits, behavior, ability to cope with difficult challenges, and religious inclination—are shaped primarily during childhood. By the example of Jesus in Luke 2:52 ("*...Jesus increased in favor with God...*"), He had a good relationship with His heavenly father, which helped Him fulfill His purpose on Earth. As a Christian parent, it is important to understand that the grace of God upon your life covers your family, and you must take hold of that grace. However, the need to lead your children into knowing this grace of God personally cannot be overemphasized.

A Christian upbringing establishes a moral and spiritual foundation in children, giving them proper spiritual direction so they will be able to withstand the storms of life. Children should be clearly taught the distinction between good and evil, right and wrong. As mentioned earlier, some parents think the spiritual upbringing of their children is the responsibility of the Sunday school teacher, the pastor, or the church in general. Yes, the church has a part to play, but it is the parents' job to teach the child spiritual truth.

> *And these words, which I command you today, shall be in your heart. You shall teach them diligently to your children, and shall talk of them when you sit in your house, when you walk by the way, when you lie down and when you rise up. You shall bind them as a sign on your hand, and they shall be as frontlets between your eyes. You shall write them on the doorposts of your house and on your gates* (Deuteronomy. 6:6–9).

This instruction was given to parents, and it is their duty to their children to utilize all available means to ensure that the children have all that is necessary for spiritual growth. It is impossible to give what you do not have, so it's very important for you as a parent to first align yourself. Where do you stand with God? All wisdom comes from God. We must give Him the chance and depend on His direction to raise our children right. Is it any wonder the scripture admonishes us thus? *"Trust in the Lord with all your heart, and lean not on your own understanding; in all your ways acknowledge Him, And He shall direct your paths"* (Proverbs. 3:5–6).

Children are very unique, and you should not handle every child the same way, so you need to trust the Lord to help you raise each of your children into what He has preordained from the beginning of creation. He has the master plan and knows the end of every man from his beginning. When I see new buildings coming up, when they are still at the foundation level nothing makes sense to me. Ordinarily, I am not able to figure out what the architect had in mind, but as they continue to build, it gradually unfolds. God is the master builder, and because He has the master plan, He is the one who will make our children what He wants them to be. But He uses people to guide them into His will and purpose, so as a parent the responsibility is yours. God expects you to be a role model to your children in the things of God. Let them see you serve God, and teach them practical Christian living and to know God for themselves. The Bible says:

> *Whom will he teach knowledge? And whom will he make to understand the message? Those just weaned from milk? Those just drawn from the breasts? For precept must be upon precept, precept upon precept. Line upon line, line upon line. Here a little, there a little"* (Isaiah 28: 9–10).

It is essential for parents to make nurturing their children's spiritual health a daily priority. Great spiritual health can be described as the state of a child's maximum well-being in a personal relationship with God. To be spiritually healthy, a child needs to be taught what a personal relationship with God is and see other people model that kind of relationship. You are the best model your child can have. When you practically involve your children in the things of God, over time those things will become part of their daily lives.

There are so many things we can do with our children to help them develop good Christian habits. I must emphasize here that you have to lead the way and show the example. Let worship be an important part of your family. Let your children see you worship and serve, and then teach them to do the same. Reading the Bible to your young children is crucial. Take time to consistently pray with your children and also give them the opportunity to pray. You will be amazed at how they will respond to your examples.

FAMILY ALTAR

Help your children develop a thirst and hunger for the word of God. Build an altar for the Lord in your home where your children are fed daily by the life-giving word of God, and then take it one step further by ensuring they have daily personal quiet time. This will foster an intimate relationship with God. More often than not, we rush out of bed in the morning, starting our day in a hurry, and then head out to work in a hurry and practically go through the day in a hurry. In the midst of all the hustling, we must find time to pray and share the word of God with our children.

I remember a particular day when we rushed out of the house in our usual hurry and forgot to pray. We had woken up late that morning, so we decided to go ahead and get ready for school/work first and then pray before leaving (instead of our usual routine of having our devotion first before anything else). Probably because it was not our usual sequence of routine, we forgot to pray after we had gotten ready. We finished having breakfast, and then we all rushed into the car as usual. I had driven about two blocks when my then five-year-old called softly, "Mummy, we forgot something." My mind quickly went to their lunches. I thought I'd forgotten their lunch boxes at home—after all, what could be more important on a school day than children's lunches? But she said, "Mummy, it's about God. We haven't prayed." I quickly apologized to them, and then we prayed right there in the car.

We've tried quite a number of strategies to ensure a consistent family devotion. Over time we were able to find a time that works for our family that we have been consistent with. If you try one way and it does not work, keep on trying other strategies. With determination, you will surely find a good time for your family.

Apart from praying with our children, we should endeavor to also read the Bible with them or to them. Teach your children the word of God and its principles; let them value the word of God, knowing that it has the answer to every question they may have. Sometimes we share the word with them and wonder if it ever makes any sense to them. The word of God is spirit. Just keep reading it to them. The Holy Spirit will then expand it in their hearts, and whenever they find themselves in a situation where they need the word, it will flow from the inside of them and provide answer for that situation.

In addition to a family altar, personal quiet time is a key part of Christian living, which children should learn early in life. It's important that they discover God for themselves. It can be difficult sometimes to find time for these things with everyone's very tight schedules, but it is possible. Try sending your children to bed about thirty minutes before their regular bedtime, and let them spend that thirty minutes in personal devotion and reflection (quiet time with God). Provide them with age-appropriate devotionals that will also give them opportunity to journal, and make sure they use them. For your children to appreciate and make sense of these principles of the word of God, you have to help them understand the basics of your faith. What does Christianity mean to you? What is your testimony? How much do you value worship, prayer, and studying God's word? These are questions you should answer as parents, as the answers will help you form spiritual values that will help you raise faith-shaped children. Once the foundation is laid, at the right time the child will himself easily make a decision for Christ, accepting him as personal Lord and Savior when the time is ripe.

THE SALVATION OF OUR CHILDREN

The greatest goal Christian parents should have for their children, is for them to accept Christ as their Lord and Savior. This is different from going to church regularly; it is a personal relationship with God. Children need to be observed for indications of their spiritual maturity and readiness to develop their faith. There is the tendency either to neglect this important aspect of your child's life or go to the other extreme and force it. However, we can't force it. All we need to do is to create the right atmosphere for our children to thrive spiritually. Make the environment in your home Christ-centered, and allow the Holy Spirit to do the work. Resolve to disciple your children, taking them by the hand and pointing them to the way of the cross.

In view of the fact that we take them to church regularly, it is easy to take their salvation for granted. Salvation is personal, and until that child consciously accepts and confesses Jesus as her personal Lord and savior, she is not saved, no matter how long she has been in church. According to the Bible, …*That if you confess with your mouth the Lord Jesus and believe in your heart that God has raised Him from the dead, you will be saved. For with the heart one believes unto righteousness, and with the mouth confession is made unto salvation* (Romans 10:9). This truth applies both to children and adults. As you make the effort to win the souls of your friend and other family members for Christ, think about winning the souls of your children for Christ as well. Do not leave it to chance! Even though I was practically raised in church, I needed to know God for myself. At about the age of twelve, after having been in church all my life, I consciously committed my heart to Christ in my Sunday school class, accepting Jesus as my personal Lord and savior, and became born again. The foundation had been laid, and I had been exposed to the word of God, which continued to water my life. Then I started to grow and mature in faith. I understood the joy of being a Christian as a teenager and living for Christ.

When our son was about six years old, he committed his heart to Christ during the Easter celebration that year. We had taken the week before Easter Sunday to read from the scriptures the story of Jesus' death and resurrection like we did every year. That year, we climaxed it with an incredible movie: *The Story of Jesus for Children.* The story was illustrated in the movie by little children, and at the end of the movie, a little boy, who was the narrator of the movie, made an altar call, asking those who wanted to accept Christ to pray the prayer of salvation. Our son quickly joined in the prayer and committed his heart to Christ. It was a very exciting moment for me, even though I wasn't sure if at that age he really knew what he was doing or whether he was just responding to the emotions of the movie. But I hoped it was the real thing, and we began to nurture it.

When he was nine years old, he attended a vacation Bible school (VBS) in the summer and responded to the call for salvation again. Before attending the VBS, he had read a book, which was the story of a girl who had faced many challenges growing up and then had the opportunity to accept Christ into her heart. He told me that she did so, not out of pressure, but because she was convinced that she needed to do it. He was touched by the story, so he answered the call to "give his life to

Christ again." Immediately, the call was made during the VBS. I asked him why he had to do that, and he said, "I have always thought that I had to be a Christian because it runs in our family, but after reading the book, I realized that I don't have to be a Christian just because we are a Christian family but because I have made up my mind to be born again."

Yes! That was the moment I had been praying for. I explained to him, though, that salvation is a personal thing and cannot be transferred. Therefore, it does not "run in our family" in that sense. By the grace of God, members of our family at one point or another have invited Christ into their hearts individually. Being a "Christian family," which is often characterized by going to church, does not mean salvation. We began to disciple him and create the right environment for him to build his faith. We went further to teach him about the "assurance of salvation." With our three children, we have had ups and downs, and as they get older, they have new experiences that draw them to the practicality of the word of God. But with the foundation laid on God's word, they are finding answers that build up their faith, and this is still a work in progress in God's hands, heading in the right direction.

Pray regularly for the salvation of your children—that they will come to a point when they will surrender their hearts to Christ as their personal Lord and savior. There is a notion that children will stumble on the word and salvation with time. Well, there is no certainty in that assumption. Although I believe that God can reach anyone at any time and at any age, I would not leave the salvation of my children to chance. Create the enabling environment, and God will meet them in His time.

FAMILY VALUES

Family values are moral principles that define your family. They are principles that are so important to your family that you adhere to them in your home. Let's distinguish between issues that are really important in the development of our children and those that are not. What values are life forming and therefore important for the future life of our children? *"Train up a child in the way he should go, and when he is old he will not depart from it"* (Proverbs. 22:6). This very popular scripture suggests that there are two ways: the way they should go and the way they should not go. And it admonishes us to help the children through the right way (the way they should go), which is the "straight and narrow way." In simple terms, look into the future: what skills, what values, and what character traits should they be developing for that journey into the future? Keeping these thoughts in mind will help you put together a set of morals: spiritual and relational values that you can build your children's foundation upon in line with God's word.

Your family values could be a combination of personal and relational values so that you do not concentrate on yourselves only but take other members of the family into consideration. This ultimately affects how they relate with others even outside their household. Here are some personal and relational values that can help form the character of our children.

MUTUAL RESPECT

Children need to learn that everyone is important and everyone deserves respect. The golden rule here is to treat others the way you would like to be treated. Respect is said to be reciprocal: when you respect yourself and other people, you will be respected as well. When there is mutual respect within a family, it creates a peaceful atmosphere in the home, and it becomes easy for the children to be respectful to others outside the home. We need to teach and model this to our children.

LOVE

Love is very important among family members. *"Love suffers long and is kind; love does not envy; love does not parade itself, is not puffed up, does not behave rudely, does not seek its own, is not provoked, thinks no evil, does not rejoice in iniquity but rejoices in the truth; bears all things, believes all things, hopes all things, endures all things"* (1 Corinthians 13:4-8). If parents succeed in building this foundation of love in their home, there will be no room for the enemy to break into that home. I know some families with adult children who are constantly at war. Siblings are against one another, and parents are at war with their children. On the other hand, I have also seen families with adult children who are always there for one another. Imagine the contrast between the two kinds of families described.

You have a duty to set the tone for love and warmth in your home. What kind of foundation are you laying? Let your children grow up to love one another, and help them to appreciate one another. When children learn to show love appropriately, this is reflected in their relationship with their friends and peers outside the home as well. Indeed, "Charity begins at home."

Family members must love one another enough to tell one another the truth, even when it is hard to do so (tough love), and also take genuine criticisms from family members in good faith. When we are able to criticize one another constructively at home, we are not likely to be easily embarrassed outside.

OBEDIENCE

God expects children to obey their parents and other authorities. Obedience is an act of love. Jesus said to his disciples in John 14:15, *"If you love me keep my commandment."* This is one way children show their love to their parents, by being obedient to them.

We must teach our children obedience and also demand it from them. Constantly use the scriptures to teach your children that God expects them to be obedient to authorities: their parents, the school, and the state. Teach your children to obey the laws/rules, and also model this to them. Do not run the red light and expect that your child will grow up to obey traffic laws (we will discuss more on instituted authorities in the next chapter). Let us teach them to do the right thing.

CARE

We should teach our children to care about what happens to other family members and people around them. When one member of the family is dealing with an issue, for example, everyone in the house should be concerned and find ways to help. This will build strong attachment among family members. Teach your children to look out for one another and also that "charity must begin at home." When they learn to care for themselves and other family members, they will be able to care for others as well.

EXCELLENCE

Encourage your children to work hard and put their best into whatever they do. We should set a standard of excellence for our children and ourselves, and we must not compromise on this. Children need to learn to work hard and also work smart in order to face the world. You should also create an enabling environment in your home for excellence by providing the resources and opportunities your children need to excel. Excellence can become a culture, and it starts with setting standards. Communicate those standards, and let them know that you have high expectations of them. They may not achieve the ultimate in one day, but there should be continuous improvement. When a child is not doing well at school, for instance, you should help him continue to improve measurably until excellence becomes a culture.

Don't always expect the change to be drastic. It is possible with some children, but for many others, it's a more gradual process. Your child might not jump from a D to an A; it is OK to see a gradual and consistent improvement in academic growth from a D to a C to a B until he gets where he should be. It is important to note that children have different abilities; therefore, not every child will be able to achieve an A. The really important thing is to build that culture of continuous improvement, which in turn sets the tone for excellence.

Excellence should not only be emphasized in academics but also in character, faith, and everything they do. When excellence becomes a culture, it affects every area of life.

FAITH

Let your children know that as a family you are a community of faith and that your faith is in Jesus Christ. If you are a Christian parent, this cannot be compromised. By practicing a lifestyle of faith, prayers, studying God's word, attending church, serving in church, and showing love to your neighbors (even those who don't share the same faith as you), your children will see the light. Teach them to model their faith and live for what they believe, without any fear of intimidation.

CONTENTMENT

As parents, we should develop a lifestyle of contentment and also teach our children the same. Contentment is a virtue, and it takes the grace of God and determination not to be carried away by unnecessary personal desires. This does not in any way mean embracing mediocrity but simply involves taking life one day at a time. Children need to learn to be happy with what they have, even if they desire more and can't have it. Lack of contentment often exposes children to immoral behaviors, including stealing, and paves the way for covetousness.

The most effective way to teach contentment to children is by example. As a contented parent, live in the moment. Don't dwell on the past but look forward to what the future will bring. They will grow up knowing that this is how to achieve happiness and fulfillment. Show your children the importance of being thankful for the little things in life, even when the bigger wishes have not materialized. Teach them to be thankful for what they do have by modeling it.

Does this mean we should not be ambitious? Definitely not. There has to be a balance, because you do want your children to learn to dream big. However, valuing each day as it comes is what makes life worth living. Opportunities often show up as you interact with your children daily; to reinforce these values, jump at it each time you find a teachable moment.

INTEGRITY

Let your "yes be *yes*" and your "no be *no*." We should value integrity and teach our children to be people of high integrity. Their yes must be yes, and their no, no. Truthfulness is a virtue that we should teach our children. It is something God cares very much about, and therefore, it should matter to us. This explains why you should insist that your son or daughter learn to tell the truth even when it hurts to do so. Our purpose here is to lay a foundation that will help us underscore a commitment to honesty in the future.

Teach your children to tell the truth at all times. Again, it is easier to teach this by modeling it. When you tell your child to tell the person at the door that you are not in when you are in fact at home, or when you are in the car with your children and you answer the phone and tell the person on the other end that you are somewhere else when you are just driving out of your driveway (essentially blaming your lateness on traffic), your children are watching.

Please note that there is a long list of values that cannot be overlooked. I have only mentioned a few. I encourage fathers and mothers to sit together and decide what values they need to promote in their homes in order to foster their family's godly beliefs. This will help give the children direction on how they see themselves, how they value spiritual things, and how they relate to people around them. Like I mentioned earlier, whatever we want our children to learn and know has to be taught. It is also important to note that everything is wrapped up in love. Our values affect the way we relate to other people. The scripture says first to love God and then your neighbor as yourself. If you love God, then you will care about others.

8

Purpose-Centered Discipline

*I think of discipline as the continual everyday process of
helping a child learn self-discipline*

—Fred Rogers

It is common to confuse discipline with punishment. Before I go on, I need to spell out the distinction between the two concepts. According to *Merriam-Webster, punishment* is "suffering, pain or loss that serves as retribution; a severe, rough or disastrous treatment." Punishment involves dealing with a person roughly or harshly, or inflicting pain as a way of imposing penalty for a fault or an offense. Punishment by this definition is not necessarily aimed at correcting; rather, the focus is on imposing penalty to make the person suffer for a wrongdoing. *Discipline,* on the other hand, is "training that corrects, molds or perfects the mental faculties or moral character" of a person. Discipline is proactive and involves training, correcting in love, frowning at wrongdoings, and sticking to your rules. Putting the two together, punishment is the consequence for lack of discipline. Discipline is the first real step toward teaching your child about the rules of life. Children should be taught and made to understand early in life that:

- They cannot always have their way: they can't do everything they want to do or have everything they want to have.
- There are boundaries, and they should stay within those defined boundaries.

Communicate to your children what these boundaries are and what the acceptable behavior is. Children need to have a clear understanding of these limits, or boundaries. They also need to know that there are consequences for their behaviors or actions. For example, a child needs to learn that a tantrum is not an acceptable behavior. Don't let your child have his way because he threw a tantrum; rather, help him learn how to present his case. The path toward establishing and enforcing discipline in children begins with parents having good boundaries and discipline (self-discipline) themselves. If we have self-discipline as parents, it becomes easy for our children to develop good discipline. We have said it before and it bears repetition that your children learn a lot from how you behave. They watch how you respond to situations, how you treat them, and how you relate to your spouse and other people, and they emulate whatever you do, good or bad.

Children are not born with self-discipline; therefore, they have to be taught. First, parents should know their children intimately to be able to provide the direction that is required. Because of immaturity, the seeming foolishness of children, and their natural tendency for rebellion, they need some guidance and control. In providing discipline, parents have to focus a great deal on the character and attitude of their children. *Character* refers to attributes or features that make up or distinguish an individual: his abilities or inabilities, his moral attributes, the way he handles relationships, and how he handles tasks in general.

It describes what a person does in certain situations and how she does it. Can she love or care for others? Can she be responsible? Does she have respect for others? Can she develop her talent and solve problems? Can she deal with failure? How does she reflect the image of God? These are some of the issues that define character.

It is a common saying that "a person's character is his destiny." This means that a person's character to a large extent determines how he will function in life. This makes it extremely necessary that you help your children mold their character, thereby preparing them for the future. When we provide discipline and help our children develop godly character, we will worry less about punishment.

PARENTAL AUTHORITY

God has established institutions of authority (chains of command), such as the government, church, home, and school, to create order in society. These institutions are designed to exercise God's authority within certain boundaries or defined limits in order to restrain the natural human tendency to exploit. The purpose of this authority is to bring control as a hindrance to open rebellion. These chains of command, or institutions of authority, are God's umbrellas of protection and instruments for the orderly administration of His plan for humankind. The point is: our authority as parents is God's way of protecting our children. It is our God-given responsibility as parents to establish this much-needed control and lead them into the way of growth and maturity, the way that gives the child true significance, satisfaction, and security, with eternal results. As part of the training process, children need to recognize, appreciate, and respond to the role of their parents in establishing control and enforcing discipline in the home. We should teach our children to understand and respect this God-given role. *"The rod and rebuke give wisdom, but a child left to himself brings shame to his mother"* (Proverbs. 29:15).

A child's rebellion can sometimes be a reflection of the parent's lack of ability or commitment to discipline and bring control into the child's life. However, there are definitely cases where parents have done all that is necessary to bring the child up in the proper way, yet this is not reflected in the child's behavior both at home and outside the home. This is where prayers come in, because parenting is not about expertise. It is really by the grace of God; it is the Holy Spirit working through you. Just keep doing all you can, but most importantly, keep sowing the seed of prayer, and someday the story will turn around.

As we exercise our God-given authority as parents, it's important to understand that God has absolute and complete authority and the right of complete control because of who He is as the sovereign Creator. Parental authority is a delegated authority, which means parents are not free to do with their children as they please. Ultimately, the authority we exercise as parents is God's authority. Children are stewardships from God, blessings He has given to parents to manage for Him. But to be good stewards, we must raise our children according to God's guidelines and authority so they come to know God and obey and behave as the children of God.

Therefore, as parents, we are required to be in a subordinate relationship to God. We are to exercise only the authority God has given us and to do so in accordance with His standards. We are never to arbitrarily establish what is right and wrong by our opinions or those of society, unless those standards are based on God's word. The parents' job is to declare what God's word says is right and to seek to promote that in their own lives and in their children's lives. When this is not the case, the parents are acting in rebellion themselves and ruining, by negative example, the stewardship God has entrusted to their care. God's word must be your standard and guide your discipline process.

THE ROD OF CORRECTION

Is there a place for the "rod" in exercising parental authority and enforcing discipline? Absolutely, the rod of correction has its place. *"Foolishness is bound up in the heart of a child. The rod of correction will drive it far from him"* (Proverbs 22:15).

There is always a controversy about the issue of using the rod (using the cane, or hitting a child) as a way of correction. Some people, especially in Western society, believe that this is child abuse. While I agree that the excessive hitting of a child with a bare hand, cane, or anything else (where it leaves bruises on the child) is a physical abuse of the child, I also believe that it is biblical to use the cane when necessary and appropriately, according to the scripture above. However, there are other equally effective forms of discipline, and we should understand that what works for one child may not necessarily work for another.

For example, while some children will only respond to the cane, there are others who respond better to "the look," "the talk," time-out, and so on. Children are different and react differently to discipline, so you need to know what form of discipline works best for your child. In my opinion, whatever strategy of correction that works for you and your child and yields the desired result becomes your "rod." It could be taking away privileges, depriving the child of some fun, or spanking with a cane. I encourage you to use the "rod" only when necessary and to not feel bad about it.

THE SEED OF PRAYER

We cannot ignore the eternal effect of praying for our children. I must say here that prayer is the most important factor in making all we have been discussing effective. We can depend on the help of the Holy Spirit to raise our children right. If we are to make a positive impact in the lives of our children and in the generation to come, we should learn to be praying parents and commit to this. You cannot underestimate the power of praying parents and much more so a parent who knows what the word of God says concerning his or her child and proclaims it. We often hear testimonies about the power of a praying mother, but a step further is when both parents (the father and mother) engage in the prayer of agreement for their children. You will be amazed at the result. I am a fruit of prayerful parenting. To date, my aged parents still wake up at a particular time in the early hours of the morning every day to pray for their children and grandchildren.

A mother recently shared with me the struggle she went through in raising her son. At the time, it looked like that child would never be responsible. She did all she knew to do to raise godly and responsible children. She had peace with her other three children, but this particular one did not give her peace. One thing she remembers, though, is that she did not stop praying. She would pray and prophesy over the life of this child, declaring the purpose of God. Today, it is a different story. She cannot explain how, but this child has graduated from the university and has become such a gentleman, loving and serving the Lord. That is what prayer can do. When you have done all you can and should do humanely, you let God do what only He can do.

The scripture says: *"Arise, cry out in the night. At the beginning of the watches: Pour out your heart like water before the face of the Lord. Lift your hands toward Him for the life of your young children who faint from hunger at the head of every street"* (Lamentation 2:19). Your children might not literally be fainting for hunger, but they may have issues with rebellion, peer pressure, academics, their faith, or other challenges that confront young people. It is only through consistent prayers that you can help them out of such situations.

"And give Him no rest, till He establishes and till He makes Jerusalem a praise in the earth" (Isaiah 62:7). I consider my children the Jerusalem in this passage. I interpret the scripture thus: "Give the Lord no rest until He establishes and makes my children a praise on earth." That should be our desire and prayer for our children. We need a lot of wisdom to survive the job of parenting, and wisdom only comes from above. The source of all true wisdom is God.

"For the Lord gives wisdom: From His mouth come knowledge and understanding" (Proverbs. 2:6). No matter the number of parenting books you've read or will read, or how many parenting seminars you attend,

you can never get all the answers to every question or solutions to every problem confronting your children and family. While these resources will definitely provide useful information and give you pointers, none will ever be absolute. You need God's help. The good thing is that God himself has offered us help according to the scriptures. *"If any of you lack wisdom, let him ask of God, who gives to all liberally and without reproach, and it will be given to him"* (James 1:5).

Purposeful parenting calls for tremendous grace, patience, strength, peace…and the list goes on and on. When we seek out the word of God that speaks to specific areas of our need and pray in faith, we can be sure that God will give us everything we need to carry through in our journey. *"Therefore I say unto you, whatever things you ask when you pray, believe that ye receive them and you will have them"* (Mark 11:24).

Prayer is the most powerful force available to us in raising our children purposefully. It is not a "piece of cake" to nurture children intellectually, physically, spiritually, and socially as we have discussed in this book, but it can be made less burdensome when we commit the journey to God in prayers every step of the way. When we pray for our children, we need to be specific. Commit their destiny to God—that He will make their paths brighter and brighter (Proverbs 4:8). It should also be our prayer that our children are filled with the Spirit of God. *"The Spirit of the Lord shall rest upon Him, the Spirit of wisdom and understanding, the Spirit of counsel and might, the Spirit of knowledge and of the fear of the Lord"* (Isaiah 11:2).

Whether you believe it or not, the devil is after your child. The word of God says that he (the devil) comes to steal, to kill, and to destroy (John 10:10a), and that he roams around the earth like a roaring lion, seeking whom he may devour (1 Peter 5:8). But the good news is that Jesus has come to give life (John 10:10b). It is only in the place of prayer that we can protect our children from the influence of the devil. God has a specific and special plan for your child, and you must stand in the gap as the gatekeeper to see that God's purpose for your child's life is fulfilled. As for me, I have made up my mind: I will not give up, and I will not give in. I will travail until God has established these beautiful ones He has given to me and made them "a praise on Earth." Prayer is the most important ingredient for purposeful parenting that can give lasting and sustainable result. Your prayer today is a seed into the future.

Let me again emphasize the need to pray for the salvation of your children. It should be the desire of every Christian parent that your child gets saved from an early age and begins to live for God. When children get saved while they are still young, they can possibly avoid mistakes they could have made ignorantly, some of which might end up subverting their course.

CONCLUSION

A s "DESTINY HELPERS" to our children, we have an inherent desire to see them fulfill their God given destinies. As we strive to parent with purpose, leading and directing our children in the way that they should go, let us not forget that *The race is not to the swift, nor the battle to the strong...* (Ecclesiastes 9:11) **it is God who gives the increase**!

As I conclude this book, here are words of encouragement to mothers and fathers. Please be encouraged as you strive to raise godly children and trust God to make them what He wants them to be.

MOTHERS

My intention in writing this book was not to overwhelm you with a sense of guilt. As I worked on this book, I had the opportunity to reflect, and as in a mirror, my inadequacies and shortcomings (the obvious areas I need to work on to fulfill my purpose in my journey and ministry of motherhood) were revealed. You may have shared this experience and seen yourself clearly from reading this book. No matter where you are and what your situation is, I want you to live above the guilt and be encouraged. God understands your situation and is able to make a way.

As mothers we find ourselves confronted with multiple roles: as a mother, wife, career woman or businesswoman, and so on. The word of God says that He will meet the desires of our heart. Will you dare trust Him today? Lay your desires and situations before Him, and trust Him to help you. While you trust God for help, think of practical ways to improve your parenting journey. Is life too busy or too complex? Perhaps a little simplification can help you find the time you never seem to have for your children or even for yourself. Sometimes we are engaged in projects and tasks that can be delegated or disregarded. We are often conditioned to think that doing more, especially at work and sometimes at the expense of our family, will lead to greater success and fulfillment. What is important is doing your best. Focus on things that are truly important, delegate when you should, and disregard the unnecessary things.

Balance is the answer. You need to find a way to balance your life, activities, and priorities so that the most important things in your life do not suffer, and this requires you to ask yourself some simple questions: "What are my priorities? What are the most important things in my life?" This may be hard to remember when the demands of work and home overwhelm you in their need for immediate attention. However, it is important to know what comes first in your life. Articulate what objectives at home and at work are most important, and be sure to plan for those first.

To keep the balancing act in motion, you should live your life according to your values and purpose. What are your values, and what is your purpose in life? Like priorities, the big idea of our own purpose in life can get lost in the day-to-day details. Is work all about making money, or is there more? Is being a parent about providing food, clothing, and shelter for your children alone, or is there more to it? If you haven't had time to think strategically about what is important and build a plan around it, now is the time to sit down and develop a plan to make your life more fulfilling and productive. If you haven't figured out the answer to the above questions, perhaps you could spend some time right away and give it a thought.

Balance is experienced differently by everyone and can be identified by some or all of the following feelings:

- the feeling of having enough time for family and work
- life "flowing" and feeling relatively effortless or stress-free

- having the resources to cope when something in your life breaks down (the nanny leaves, the car breaks down, the driver does not show up, and so on)
- being on the path you desire personally and professionally for the future

Balance is usually not constant. It fluctuates as things change in life, and it has to be worked at. You need to consciously make the effort to create the needed balance. Life is about the choices we make. Above everything, you must depend on the unending grace of God: *"It is God who works in you both to will and to do for His good pleasure"* (Philippians 2:13).

FATHERS

Fathers play a fundamental role in the life of their children. They matter a lot and have a huge influence on their children's development. It is important that fathers realize how their relationship with their children affects their self-esteem, how well they do at school, and even whether they are able to form happy, long-lasting relationships as adults. This is all highly influenced by this father-child relationship. The more time fathers spend with their children, the greater the impact. Even though as the father and breadwinner of your household, you may be understandably busy (even extremely so), it's imperative that you make time in your busy schedule to bond and connect with your children. Fathers need quality time with their children; it's not necessarily about the length of time spent with the children but the quality of time.

Your son especially needs a man who is active in his life and can teach him how to be a man, modeling real manhood to him. He needs someone to talk to and share his fear and hopes with. Boys need to learn from their fathers how to be good husbands, fathers, and citizens. They need to learn to love the Lord and assume the God-ordained position of being the head of the home. They should be taught proper grooming as well.

Likewise, your wife also needs you around to bring perspective to issues. With my husband and our son, I realized that there were successes I couldn't have achieved with our son without his dad. I tend to overreact sometimes, but when my husband reassures me that certain things are common with boys and even shares his own experiences and how he overcame them, it gives perspective to issues and situations.

What can I say about the fascinating love between fathers and their daughters? Your daughters need you also. The benefit of having an active father in their lives cannot be overemphasized. You are a key figure in the development of your daughter's view of a good man. The well-fathered daughters or daughters who perceive that their fathers care a lot about them, and who feel emotionally connected to their fathers are more balanced emotionally and are less likely to exhibit a low self-esteem or be easily swayed by deception.

Finally, Life is a long walk, and so is parenting. For me, the journey continues as I am now in another stage of my parenting journey: the teenage years. Soon we will be sharing these experiences in the sequel to *Purposeful Parenting.*

I pray that you will find the strength, wisdom, and grace to take this long walk in fulfillment of the purpose of God for your life and the lives of your children. God is the designer, and He has created your child for a purpose. May the Lord help you to fulfill your role in your child's life and destiny and may He reward your labor over your children with His peace.

BIBLIOGRAPHY

Carson, Ben. *Gifted Hands: The Ben Carson Story*. Grand Rapids: Zondervan, 1990.

CDC. "Childhood Obesity Facts." Last modified August 27, 2015. http://www.cdc.gov/healthyyouth/obesity/facts.htm

Davies, Martin. *The Blackwell Encyclopedia of Social Work*. Malden: Wiley, 2000.

First Five Sonoma County. "Speaking for Children: The Early Years." Last modified April 2009.http://www.first5sonomacounty.org/documents/newsletters/english/the_early_years.pdf

HelpGuide.org. "Nutrition for Children and Teens." Maya W. Paul and Lawrence Robertson. Last modified February 2016. http://helpguide.org/articles/healthy-eating/nutrition-for-children-and-teens.htm

Livestrong.com. "How Poor Nutrition Affects Child Development." Dakota Karratti. Last modified on April 24, 2015. http://www.livestrong.com/article/465374-how-poor-nutrition-affects-child-development/

Lush, Jean, and Pamela Vrendevelt. *Mothers and Sons: Raising Boys to Be Men*. Grand Rapids: Revell, 2001.

Mayo Clinic. "Nutrition for Kids: Guidelines for a Healthy Diet." Last modified January 16, 2016. http://www.mayoclinic.org/healthy-lifestyle/childrens-health/in-depth/nutrition-for-kids/art-20049335

Medical-Dictionary.com. "Growth." Last modified on December 3, 2013. http://www.medical-dictionary.thefreedictionary.com/growth

www.ingramcontent.com/pod-product-compliance
Lightning Source LLC
Chambersburg PA
CBHW051733040426
42447CB00008B/1110

* 9 7 8 0 6 9 2 6 5 3 3 9 5 *